TARA
THE GUIDEBOOK

Mairéad Carew

The Discovery Programme: Centre for
Archaeology and Innovation Ireland,
63 Merrion Square, Dublin 2, Ireland
www.discoveryprogramme.ie

ISBN 978-0-9536973-2-8

Text: Mairéad Carew
Design and layout: Ian McCarthy
Cover Design: Ian McCarthy
Illustrations: Annie West

The Discovery Programme would like to acknowledge
the financial assistance received from the
Office of Public Works and the Heritage Council
towards the publication of this guidebook.

Printed by GPS Colour Graphics Ltd,
Alexander Road, Belfast BT69HP, Northern Ireland

'I mean the traces on Tara are in the grass, are in the earth – they aren't spectacular like temple ruins would be in the Parthenon in Greece but they are about origin, they're about beginning, they're about the mythological, spiritual source – a source and a guarantee of something old in the country and something that gives the country its distinctive spirit.'

Seamus Heaney, poet and Nobel Laureate

Contents

1: Royal Tara

2: The monuments

3: Tara in medieval times

3: Tara in medieval times (cont'd)

4: Politics, protests and plans

5: The study of Tara

Preface

Tara is a sacred prehistoric burial site and a very important landscape in the psyche and imagination of the Irish people. The oldest monument on the hill, the Mound of the Hostages, was built in the Neolithic period and was later reused as an early Bronze Age cemetery. Large ritual monuments were constructed in the Iron Age.

In the medieval period Tara was an important site politically because of its association with kingship. In later centuries, it retained its potency and became the site of hostings, battles and assemblies. To cultural nationalists in the nineteenth century, Tara was the capital of an independent Ireland and was described by W.B. Yeats as 'the most consecrated spot in Ireland'.

To dreamers in the twentieth century Tara could be restored to its former glory. In the twenty-first century a threat to the cultural integrity of the site by a proposed motorway became the focus of much debate. Tara, a unique cultural landscape with its archaeological monuments, history and place in folklore and literature, will continue to fascinate people into the future.

The Discovery Programme
Centre for Archaeology
and Innovation Ireland

The Discovery Programme, an all-island centre for archaeology and heritage science, was established in 1991. The organization's primary aims are to benefit the community by advancing research in Irish archaeology along with other disciplines such as archival studies, history and modern technology, and sharing this knowledge with a wide range of audiences. The Discovery Programme has been conducting research into Tara and its landscape since 1991 and this work is continuing. *Tara: the guidebook* explains our current understanding of this immensely complex site in an accessible and entertaining format.

Map of Tara complex

Over one hundred archaeological sites have been discovered on the Hill of Tara. The majority of these have been revealed through non-invasive technology such as geophysical survey. The remains of over thirty monuments are visible in the Tara complex. This ritual site consists of the Hill of Tara (A–S), and monuments situated in the wider landscape (T–Y).

A Site entrance

B Statue of St Patrick

C St Patrick's Church

D Adomnán's Cross

E The Banqueting Hall

F Rath Gráinne

G Northern Clóenfherta

H Southern Clóenfherta

I Henge/ditched pit circle

J Rath of the Synods

Lia Fáil and 1798 Memorial

Mound of the Hostages

Adomnán's Cross

K Mound of the Hostages

L Ráith na Rí

M The Forrad

N 1798 Memorial

O The Lia Fáil

P Tech Cormaic

Q Ráith Lóegaire

R Nemhnach (sacred spring)

S Rath Meave

T Ringlestown Rath

U Riverstown linear earthwork

V Rath Miles

W Lismullin

X Rath Lugh

Y Skreen

Ráith Gráinne (top), Northern Clóenfherta (Left) and Southern Clóenfherta (Right)

Hill of Tara and sites in surrounding landscape

M3

Rath Miles   Lismullin   Rath Lugh

Skreen

Riverstown linear earthwork   Hill of Tara

Ringlestown Rath   Rath Maeve

Neolithic period (4000–2500BC)

Great Pyramid of Giza completed 2600

Newgrange constructed 3200–3100

Céide Fields, Co. Mayo, 3700–3200

Henge monument/ditched pit circle built c.2500

Mound of the Hostages built c.3500

Banqueting Hall

Early Bronze Age cemetery, Mound of the Hostages

Stonehenge, 2200–1800

Viking period

Early medieval period (AD400–800)

Gormlaith married Brian Ború

Brian Ború became King of Cashel, 978

Tara Brooch, c.700

St Patrick arrives in Ireland, 432

Battle of Clontarf, 1014

Queen Lann buried three husbands, all kings, in the ninth century; died 890

Abbot Adomnán of Iona, 679–704

Last celebration of *Feis Temro*, 560

Diarmait mac Cerbaill, King of Tara, 544–565

Maél Sechlainn mac Domnaill, King of Tara, 979–1022

Gormlaith married Máel Sechlainn mac Domnaill, 981

Battle of Tara, 980

Early modern Ireland

Late medieval period

Dindshenchas of Tara, *Book of Leinster*, 12th century

Hugh O'Neill rallied troops at Tara before Battle of Kinsale, 1601

Battle of Tara, 1798

Building o church at Tara, 182

Foundation of church at Tara by Hospitallers of St John, 1230

Meeting of rebels at Tara, 1641

Battle of the Boyne, 1690

Timeline of Tara, 4000BC–AD2016

Bronze Age (2500–500BC)

Tara Torcs, 1200–1000

Tara 'Boy-King', 1700–1600

Tara workshop: Iron Age bronze working, Ráith na Rí

Iron Age (500BC–AD400)

Building of Lismullin temple, Middle Iron Age

Julius Caesar attacks Britain, 55BC

Iron Age Temple at Navan Fort built 95–94 BC

Evidence for habitation, Rath of the Synods, AD200–300

Birth of Jesus Christ

Roman objects, Rath of the Synods, 1st–4th century AD

Ráith na Rí, c.AD100

Reading of the proclamation, 2016

Discovery Programme Tara Project 1991–present

William O'Donnell's plans for Tara, 1970s

M3 controversy and excavations, 2002–2010

Tara Broadcast by R.A.S. Macalister, 1937

First scientific excavations by UCD professors S.P. Ó Ríordáin and Ruaidhrí de Valera, 1950s

New city of Tara plans by Daithí Ó hÁinle, 1942

Lia Fáil moved from Mound of the Hostages to Forrad to commemorate 1798 rebels, 1824

Daniel O'Connell's Monster Meeting at Tara, 1843

British Israelite excavations at Tara, 1899–1902

Tara: a pagan sanctuary of ancient Ireland by R.A.S. Macalister published 1931

Independent Ireland

Waterhouse presented Queen Victoria with replica of Tara brooch, 1850

First interdisciplinary study of Tara by George Petrie published, 1839

Modern Ireland

1: Royal Tara

What is Tara?

Tara is an important archaeological site in Ireland and worldwide. The use of the site spans from prehistory to the present. Monuments range in date from approximately 3500BC to AD400 (the Neolithic to the early medieval period) and reflect the multi-period nature of the Tara landscape. The site was mainly used in prehistory for ritual and religious purposes and as a cemetery, but there is also evidence for settlement. Monuments include a cursus, a passage tomb, barrows, a henge and other ritual enclosures, standing stones and also some natural features such as streams and springs.

Where did Tara get its name?

Tara was regarded as a sanctuary from an early period. The English version, *Tara*, comes from the Old Irish *Temair*, that has at its root, *tem*, meaning 'to cut' or 'to set apart'. This refers to a space cut off for sacred purposes. *Temair* is also related to the Greek word *temenos* meaning a sacred place defined by a ditch, boundary stones or an enclosing wall and to the Latin word *templum*, meaning 'sacred precinct'.

Who built Tara?

The ordinary people who lived in the landscape at the time the monuments were constructed built Tara. Tara during prehistory must have been at the centre of power as it had an organising force that could get able-bodied men to spend months (and in some cases, years) building the monuments. The fact that the monuments were used over a long period of time suggests that there must have been a stable society in prehistory in the vicinity of Tara. The funerary nature of the monuments and the extent of the ritual landscape suggest a settled agricultural community. Farmers, rooted in the landscape, intended to stay. They built monuments to last and to serve as a permanent marker of their presence. They buried their dead there and watched or participated in rituals being performed.

A prayer to the cosmos

The ritual of building and using the monuments was a prehistoric prayer to the cosmos. This prayer was to ward off or delay the destructive powers of nature, which included bad harvests, sickness and death. The rituals performed at Tara acknowledged the fragility of life and man's vulnerability in the face of the forces of nature.

These monuments in the landscape acted as focal points and reassured the community of their safety in a precarious world, provided that the gods were appeased and the harvest was good.

A prehistoric royal site

Tara is considered to be one of the great prehistoric royal sites of Ireland. These also include Navan Fort, Co. Armagh, Rathcroghan, Co. Roscommon, Uisneach, Co. Westmeath and Knockaulin, Co. Kildare. Some archaeologists believe the description 'royal' was retrospectively applied to these sites because of the way they were described in the medieval period. In medieval literature, Navan Fort was associated with the kings of Ulster, Rathcroghan with the kings of Connacht and Knockaulin with the kings of Leinster. Tara was reputed to be the seat of the high kings of Ireland. According to tradition, the Hill of Uisneach was the navel of Ireland and the point where the five provinces met.

All of the royal sites are located in elevated positions with panoramic views of the surrounding landscape. They are the focal points of wider archaeological landscapes containing many ritual and burial monuments. These royal sites have archaeological features in common and their architecture shows that they were clearly places of assembly where large ceremonial events took place, where knowledge of astronomy was expressed and royal inaugurations may have taken place. Megalithic tombs, Bronze Age barrows and Iron Age enclosures are found in all these landscapes.

Navan Fort, Co. Armagh

Rathcroghan, Co. Roscommon

Uisneach, Co. Westmeath

Knockaulin, Co. Kildare

Tara: the centre of the world

Royal sites are very important in Irish history and culture and feature in many myths and legends. They are also important sacred sites. Each was an *axis mundi* that was the centre of the world for their communities and the place of connection between the natural world and the Otherworld. Each site represented this idea for those involved in the construction and use of the original monuments and for those who built new monuments on the sites and continued to use them for ritual purposes down through the ages.

The *axis mundi* is the spot where the world began. Sometimes this symbol is in the form of a natural feature such as a mountain, rock or tree and sometimes it is man-made such as a maypole, pillar or spire. This symbol can be found in cultures worldwide and in major world religions; it represents a centre of safety and order. Outside its orbit is the unfamiliar and the dangerous.

Royal sites represented the centre of the world for their communities. They were significant as the places where the Otherworld could be accessed, and even more importantly, the place where ancestors were buried.

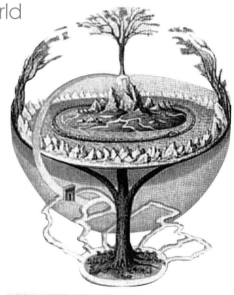

The *axis mundi* was 'the centre of the world'

Why were the ancestors important?

Venerating the ancestors is based on the belief that the dead continue, paradoxically, to have a life. The ancestors were believed to be able to intercede on behalf of the living to influence the gods. Their veneration was also important in terms of reaffirming family ties.

Ancestor veneration was not only important in Ireland in the past but also in countries across the globe. This human activity of respecting the dead is practiced down to the present day, regardless of the sophistication of the society. Even in modern times, the visiting of graves and the veneration of the dead on All Souls Day, in early November, continues in Ireland.

Tara of the kings?

Tara, as a sacred ancestral place, was deemed a worthy location for the inauguration of kings. The office of sacred king was a common idea worldwide. In Irish and many other cultures he was considered to be semi-divine and physically perfect. He was married symbolically to the land and his participation in ceremonies in the ritual landscape was essential to its fertility and necessary to the well-being of the community. It was also important because it gave people a sense of belonging and the illusion of control over their lives.

Sacral kingship

The inauguration of a sacral king took place at a prehistoric site. He became 'king of the world' and Tara was the 'centre of the world'. He presided over the sacral landscape of Tara with its monuments of different periods. This connected the present with the past, reasserting the religious and political potency of Tara. According to some scholars, these royal sites were not simply places used for the inauguration of kings, they were also places where the ritual creation of the world was re-enacted.

Architecture of inauguration

The architecture of inauguration can be seen in the structure and arrangement of the great monuments of Tara including the Banqueting Hall, Ráith na Rí and the Mound of the Hostages. This statement of power, initially expressed in the prehistoric period, was reasserted through medieval rituals of kingship.

The king and the Otherworld

The king was perceived as having a foot in the natural world and a foot in the Otherworld. The ability to cross the threshold to the Otherworld and to return safely was the preserve of the few; those communicating with the ancestors were powerful people in the community. The king of Tara became the most powerful king in Ireland. Tara, as a space between worlds, was the place to access power.

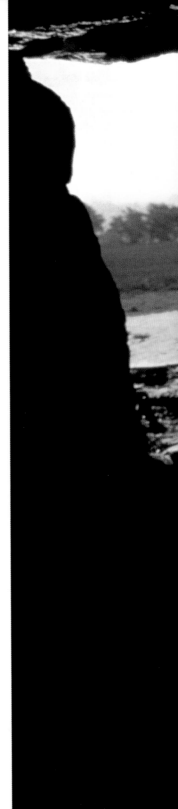

Were there kings of Tara in prehistory?

The earliest monuments on Tara date to the Neolithic period, the Bronze Age and the early Iron Age at a time when there were no written sources. Therefore, it is not possible to prove that there were kings of Tara in prehistory. This does not mean, however, that the kings did not exist. It is certainly possible to infer that there were very powerful rulers living in the Tara landscape because of the existence of the monuments.

The construction of this ritual landscape depended on those with a knowledge of the natural world, engineering and astronomy to establish the place of the community in the landscape.

Myths and prehistoric kings

The medieval sources contain stories about gods and goddesses of Tara, mythological kings and queens and also historical personages. Stories and myths are rooted in the landscape, through place-names and descriptions. There are many tales with the monuments as motifs. Stories are retold by each successive generation. They serve not just as memory aids but as a way of ensuring continuity.

Sometimes a creative story contains an essential truth about man's place in the world. An insight into the beliefs of prehistoric peoples and the meaning that the monuments had in their lives can be gleaned. A view of the land as sacred and rituals enacted to ensure its fertility were an act of self-preservation. A good harvest meant survival.

Window into an older belief system

It is clear that the study of Irish prehistory fascinated the medieval Irish and provided a window into an older belief system. Rituals re-enacted preserved tradition and were a reflection on the deep mysteries of life.

The monuments, which reflected prehistoric beliefs about the cosmos, remained in the landscape for millennia and were, in some cases, reused in later periods.

View from inside of the Mound of the hostages

Famous legendary kings of Tara

Famous legendary kings of Tara included Conaire Mór, Cormac mac Airt, Conn of the Hundred Battles and Niall of the Nine Hostages. Mythological tales detail their heroic exploits and explain the role of the king in society and how the institution of kingship itself was more important than the individual king.

Conaire's birth

The circumstances of Conaire's birth were magical. His mother was impregnated by an Otherworldly figure who appeared to her in the guise of a bird. She was told that her son must not kill birds. However, Conaire later pursued a flock of birds but they turned on him and shed their birdskins. They were revealed to be warriors with spears and swords. Their leader instructed him to go to Tara where he would become king.

King Conaire of Tara and his taboos

A king's taboos were rules that he must observe in order to keep the kingship and avoid disaster. They served as a contract with the Otherworld. Conaire Mór had the following taboos placed on him for the duration of his kingship of Tara:

i   The sun should not rise while he is in bed in the plain of Tara

ii   The sun should neither set nor rise on him in Tara

iii   He should not go righthand-wise around Tara

iv   He should not go lefthand-wise around Brega

"COME BACK! WE'RE ACTUALLY PEOPLE"

v	The evil beasts of Cerna (swans) must not be hunted by him	**ix**	Three Reds shall not go before him into a Red's house
vi	He must not go out every ninth night beyond Tara	**x**	No raiding shall be done in his reign
vii	He must not sleep in a house from which firelight is visible after sunset	**xi**	After sunset a company of one woman or one man shall not enter the king's house
viii	He must not sleep in a house in which light is visible from outside	**xii**	He shall not settle the quarrel of his two slaves

The breaking of the king's taboos

Conaire broke his taboos one after the other. He failed to exact retribution from his foster brothers who had been involved in raiding. When he eventually took action, he spared his own foster brothers but condemned their companions to death. He recognized the unfairness of this decision, revoked it and ordered the raiders to be banished to Britain. This decision violated the 'king's truth'. He failed to prevent three horsemen wearing red tunics, carrying red weaponry and riding red horses, to go before him to Da Derga's hostel. He died in a bloody confrontation there.

The king's truth

The idea of the 'king's truth' is an important element in sacral kingship. The just king guaranteed the order of the cosmos which meant:

· Prosperity and fertility for man, animals and crops

· Temperate seasons

· Corn growing strong and heavy

· Fruit abundant on the trees

· Cattle yielding plenty of milk

· Rivers and estuaries teeming with fish

· Plagues, famines and natural calamities warded off

· Internal peace and victory over external enemies

The white mare

Horses, especially white mares, were associated with early Irish kingship. This reflected the Indo-European tradition that associated sacral kingship with horses and horse sacrifice. This was a ceremony of initiation for the king. Lagore, the lake residence of the early medieval kings of South Brega got its name, *Loch da Gabor* meaning 'lake of the two white mares,' from the mythological story about the drowning of two horses there. The name of the Gabhra river, which runs through the Tara/Skreen valley, is probably also linked to a white mare.

" WE'VE A SPECIAL ON HORSE BONES ALL THIS WEEK '

The king and the horse goddess

The cult of the horse was strong in early Ireland. There are links between the cult of horses, kingship rites and goddesses throughout early Irish literature.

A sacrifical white mare
(Translation)

A white mare is brought forward into the middle of the assembly. He who is to be inaugurated, not as a chief, but as a beast, not as a king, but as an outlaw, embraces the animal before all, professing himself to be a beast also. The mare is then killed immediately, cut up in pieces and boiled in water.

A bath is prepared for the man afterwards in the same water. He sits in the bath surrounded by all his people, and all, he and they, eat of the meat of the mare which is brought to them. He quaffs and drinks of the broth in which he is bathed, not in any cup, or using his hand, but just dipping his mouth into it round about him. When this unrighteous rite has been carried out, his kingship and dominion has been conferred.

Description above written by Gerald of Wales in the 12th century Topographica Hiberniae.

Were horses eaten in ritual feasts at Tara?

Horse bones were found in the cuttings made in the ditch of the great enclosure on the Hill of Tara, Ráith na Rí, during excavations in 1997. Many of the bones were broken for the purpose of extracting the marrow. Both young and old horses were represented. Horses were generally consumed when they were mature and no longer useful.

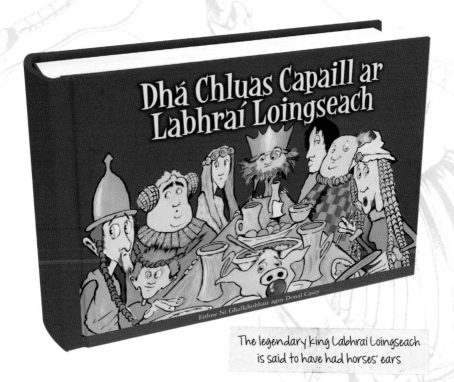

Dhá Chluas Capaill ar Labhraí Loingseach

Eithne Ní Ghallchobhair agus Dónal Casey

The legendary king Labhraí Loingseach is said to have had horses' ears

Horse burials

Horse burials have been found across Europe, dating from prehistory to the Viking period. This demonstrates the prestige or religious significance of horses. A female burial, dating to the fifth or sixth century, was found inserted into a Bronze Age mound which contained a cinerary urn at Farta, Co. Galway. The woman was accompanied by antler bones and the complete skeleton of a horse. This burial was located 500m away from the original location of the famous Iron Age Turoe Stone. It is likely that this woman was of high, even royal, status.

Cormac mac Airt

The legendary Cormac Mac Airt, grandson of Conn of the Hundred Battles, was banished to the Hill of Skreen after he was blinded in one eye. A blemished king could not gain the kingship of Tara. Cormac supposedly ruled Tara in the second or third century AD.

The wise judgement of Cormac mac Airt

The sheep of a herdswoman named Benna wandered into the queen's field and ate a crop of woad (a plant used to obtain blue dye). King Lugaid mac Con decided that the sheep had to be forfeited by their owner because of the loss of the crop and given to the queen.

Cormac mac Airt stepped forward and gave his judgement that the wool of the sheep should be given in compensation because the woad would grow back and so would the wool. This was deemed to be the wise judgement of the rightful king of Tara.

Inauguration of Cormac mac Airt

The inauguration of a 'world king' is what ensured that natural order remained in balance. During Cormac's reign the land was fertile, the harvests were plentiful, the rivers were full of fish and there was an abundance of honey. He was said to have rebuilt the ramparts of Tara and enlarged the great banqueting hall.

Cormac died after choking on a salmon bone. He was different from earlier kings of Tara in that he did not want to be buried in Brú na Bóinne, the traditional burial place of Tara's kings, but insisted on being buried in Rosnaree, on the bank of the River Boyne opposite Knowth.

Cormac: the perfect king

The beauty of the unblemished king of Tara, Cormac mac Airt, was described in the story *Scél na Fír Flatha* in the fourteenth-century *Book of Ballymote*. In this text it was written that Cormac had a body which was as white as snow. He had golden plaited hair. His lips were like a woven cord of red Parthian leather and his cheeks were like mountain foxglove. His eyes were like bluebells and his eyebrows and lashes were like the radiance of bright raven blue.

Cormac, who was renowned for his wisdom, was described in his youth as 'a listener in the woods and a gazer at the stars'.

Queen Ciarnait

Ciarnait was the lover of Cormac Mac Airt. She was the kidnapped daughter of a Pictish king and became a slave at Cormac's court. According to the *Banshenchas (Lore of women)* Ciarnait was the mother of Coirpre Lifechair, son of Cormaic mac Airt. Ciarnait was cruelly treated by Eithne, a Leinster princess and Cormac's wife. She was grinding nine bushels of corn each day using a handmill. After she became pregnant her labours became impossible.

Cormac sent for a millwright from across the sea and he built the first water-powered mill in Ireland to ease her workload. The mill was said to be situated on Nemnach, a sacred spring located at the southern end of the field containing Ráith Lóegaire.

The god Lug and the rightful king of Tara

Lug was the most important god associated with Tara. It was believed that when his voice was heard through the stone known as the Lia Fáil it confirmed the presence of the rightful king of Tara. When Conaire drove his chariot towards the two stones known as Blocc and Bluigne, they parted for him. The Lia Fáil screeched against the chariot axle. This sound, the voice of Lug, validated a man's right to the kingship of Tara.

Lug's arrival at Tara

There is a story about Lug who, on his arrival at Tara, was asked by the doorkeeper 'what art do you practice, for no one without an art enters Tara'. Lug replied that he was a builder, a smith, a champion, a harper, a warrior, a poet, a historian, a sorcerer, a physician, a cupbearer and a brazier. He said 'ask the king whether he has one man who possesses all these arts: if he has I will not be able to enter Tara'. Fidchell boards were brought to Lug and he won all the games. After that the doorkeeper let him pass.

Lug was challenged to pick up a flagstone that took eighty oxen to move and he picked it up and threw it into the centre of the royal Banqueting Hall. Lug played the harp and put his hosts to sleep. The next day he played sorrowful music so that they were crying and lamenting. When he played joyful music they were happy and rejoicing. The incumbent King Núada decided to change seats with Lug and Lug then occupied the seat of the king.

'Lugh rides to battle' (Jim Fitzpatrick)

Was Lug buried at Tara?

Lug was not buried at Tara but reputedly in a mound called Carn Lugdach at the royal site of Uisneach. This was after he was wounded in one foot and drowned in the pond there during an assembly.

A 'Celtic chess set' based on the game of Fidchell played by the god Lug

Queens and sovereignty goddesses

In early medieval literature legendary queens, such as Medb, Eithne and Temair were associated with the major prehistoric ceremonial centres. There was a pre-Christian tradition of representing the land as a female deity and the queens, deemed to be sovereignty goddesses, were personifications of this idea. The role of the sovereignty goddess in the stories was to test the candidate to see if he was the rightful king. If successful a sacred union between the ruler and the goddess followed.

There are a number of queens mentioned in medieval sources that are associated with Tara. These sources include the *Cycle of the Kings*, genealogies, the *Banshenchas* and the *Annals*. The first entries in the *Annals* for royal women was in the seventh century. By the mid-eighth century there were references to queens of Tara. The *Banshenchas*, compiled in the late twelfth century, is the most important source for pre-Norman queens. It is a catalogue starting with Eve. Eight versions of the prose *Banshenchas* are found in the *Book of Lecan* (late fourteenth to early fifteenth century).

The queens are usually mentioned in the context of their role as consorts. Queens include legendary women, daughters of historical figures and real characters in fictional stories. Queens were sometimes depicted as partners of a whole series of kings. The king was legitimized by marrying the widow of a previous king. As in other cultures, such as that of the Anglo-Saxons, political alliances as a basis for marriage among the powerful was the norm.

Maeve and mead

Maeve Lethderg of Tara was a goddess who bestowed sovereignty on kings during a ritual involving the drinking of mead. The old Irish version of the name Maeve is related to a word meaning 'strong, intoxicating one'.

What is mead?

Mead is an alcoholic beverage made by fermenting honey with water, sometimes with a variety of spices, fruits and grains. Hops are also used and act as a preservative. The alcoholic content varies from about 8% to 20% or more. Mead can be still or sparkling, dry or sweet. It is believed that mead was one of the first fermented drinks and it is mentioned in ancient sources from Europe, Asia and Africa.

The drink of sovereignty

As his sovereignty was sanctioned by the Otherworld, the rightful king had to fulfil his side of the bargain. He had to have the blessing of the goddess and she bestowed the drink of sovereignty. He was required to make righteous judgements and to preside over a peaceful kingdom. Of course, the goddess who sleeps with the king and hands him a drink of sovereignty may also turn against him. The goddess of sovereignty was, sometimes, also the goddess of death.

A king's threefold death

Sacral kings sometimes suffered a threefold death, which involved wounding, fire and drowning. For example, Muirchertach mac Erca, king of Tara, who died in AD536, was crushed by a falling roof beam, burned and drowned in a vat of wine on the eve of Samhain.

'THAT'S PRETTY GOOD MEAD, IN FAIRNESS'

Sadb: daughter of Conn of the Hundred Battles

Sadb was the daughter of the famous king of Tara, Conn of the Hundred Battles. Conn was the legendary ancestor of various historical dynasties including the Connachta and the Uí Néill. One of the great sacred trees of Ireland, a great oak that once stood in County Kildare, appeared at the time of Conn's birth. This was described as 'an offshoot of the tree in Paradise' from the Garden of Eden.

According to the thirteenth-century *Agallamh na Senórach*, Sadb, Conn's daughter, was one of the six best women in the world after Mary, the mother of God. Her importance lay in her roles as a legendary queen, sovereignty goddess, king's lover, king's mother and founder of dynasties. She was also the wife of the hero Fionn mac Cumhaill.

Sadb: sovereignty goddess and wife of Fionn mac Cumhaill (Jim Fitzpatrick)

Designed to impress

The architecture of Tara, as well as other royal sites, was designed to impress, to dominate the landscape and to demonstrate the power of man over nature. Myths and stories about gods and goddesses and kings and queens associated with these places reflect their importance. The sacredness of the king reflected the sacredness of the landscape itself.

Did the kings of Tara wear gold torcs?

Two gold torcs dating to the Middle Bronze Age (1200–1000BC) were found in the Rath of the Synods in 1810. The Tara torcs are considered to be the finest of their class in Ireland and are part of the National Museum of Ireland's prehistoric gold collection, which is the largest and most important in western Europe.

The torcs were made from gold bars twisted around each other with great skill. The craftsman clearly had the required expertise and knowledge of this precious metal. These ornaments are exceptionally large: if untwisted the larger of the torcs would extend to 1.67m. This suggests that it might have been worn around the waist, perhaps during a ritual at Tara. The use of this amount of gold points to the high status and spiritual power of the wearer.

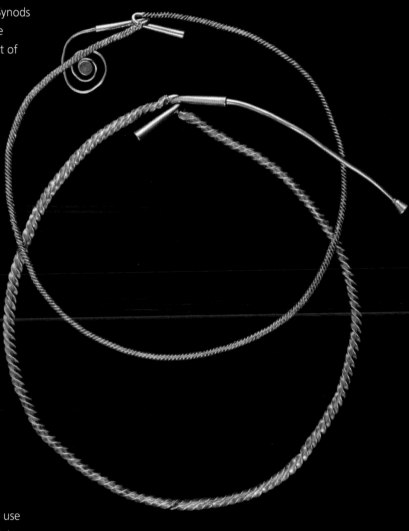

Two gold torcs found at the Rath of the Synods

Did prehistoric kings wear golden shoes?

Gold shoe fittings were found in the grave of a tall adult male in an Iron Age burial at Hochdorf in Germany. In Irish and Welsh tradition golden shoes were a symbol of kingship.

The Hochdorf man lay stretched out on a bronze couch. He had a four-wheeled wagon, horse equipment, tools and personal ornaments. He also had a drinking and feasting set that included nine drinking horns. A large bronze cauldron that had once contained mead and a golden cup were placed at his feet.

Gold shoes from the royal burial at Hochdorf in Germany

In the Irish story *The vision of the spectre*, the goddess of sovereignty offers a drink to Conn of the Hundred Battles to grant him the kingship of Tara.

The goldwork found at Hochdorf, which included a sheet gold collar, suggests that he was of high status and, possibly, a sacral king.

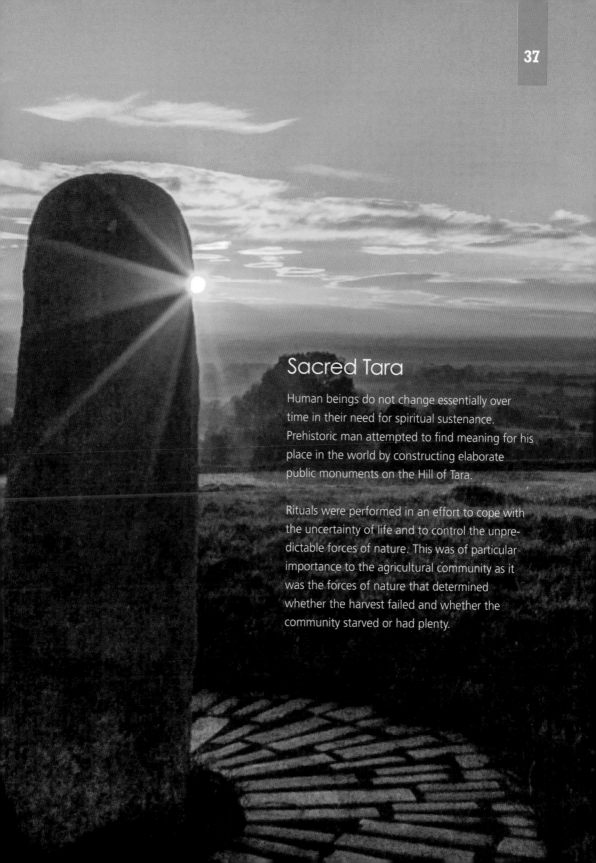

Sacred Tara

Human beings do not change essentially over time in their need for spiritual sustenance. Prehistoric man attempted to find meaning for his place in the world by constructing elaborate public monuments on the Hill of Tara.

Rituals were performed in an effort to cope with the uncertainty of life and to control the unpredictable forces of nature. This was of particular importance to the agricultural community as it was the forces of nature that determined whether the harvest failed and whether the community starved or had plenty.

2: The monuments

The Banqueting Hall

Cursus monuments, like the Banqueting Hall, consist of a pair of parallel banks that can extend over considerable distances. Some banks have ditches and some are closed at the end by terminals that are U-shaped or rectilinear. These monuments are found in Britain and Ireland. The longest one, in Dorset, is 10km in length and 100m in width. Some are located beside famous archaeological sites such as Newgrange and Stonehenge. They are among the oldest monumental structures in the world.

The term 'cursus' was first applied to this type of monument at Stonehenge in the eighteenth century by William Stukeley, an antiquarian. He interpreted it as a Roman racecourse. In Britain they have been found to date from the Neolithic period (c.4000 to c.2500BC).

There has been little research or excavation of cursus monuments in Ireland and the function of these unusual monuments has been speculated about since the medieval period. However, the likelihood is that the Irish examples are similar in function and in date to their English counterparts, even though they tend to be shorter and many do not have ditches.

Prehistoric pathway

Most cursus monuments form part of wider ritual landscapes and are associated with passage tombs, henges, barrows and other ritual monuments. It is likely that they were used as pathways for prehistoric processions, funerary events, festivals and inauguration ceremonies.

Restricted views

The situation of cursus monuments and their architecture meant that the views of the surrounding landscape were restricted. It was not until the summit was reached that the full ritual landscape was revealed. Often the cursus appears to stop short of this visual threshold.

Alignment with passage tomb

Some cursus monuments in Ireland are aligned with passage tombs. At Tara, the Banqueting Hall is aligned with the Mound of the Hostages. It extends as far as the perimeter of the prehistoric wooden henge (c.2500BC), a monument no longer visible in the landscape.

The Banqueting Hall also has different structural features to the typical cursus – the enclosed area was created by scooping soil outwards from the centre to form a broad bank on either side. This is also the case in the example at Newgrange.

Banqueting Hall

The cursus monument was essential to prehistoric ritual performed at Tara

Comparable cursus monuments: Newgrange

The cursus monument at Newgrange has parallel banks and ditches and a U-shaped terminal. It is part of a ritual landscape associated with henges, pit circles, mounds and megalithic tombs.

The Newgrange cursus is c.20m wide, 100m long and aligned north–south

Stonehenge

The Stonehenge Cursus in Wiltshire dates to the Neolithic period and predates the construction of Stonehenge. It is surrounded by barrows and is part of a wider ritual landscape.

The Stonehenge Cursus is 3km long, 100–150m wide and aligned east–west

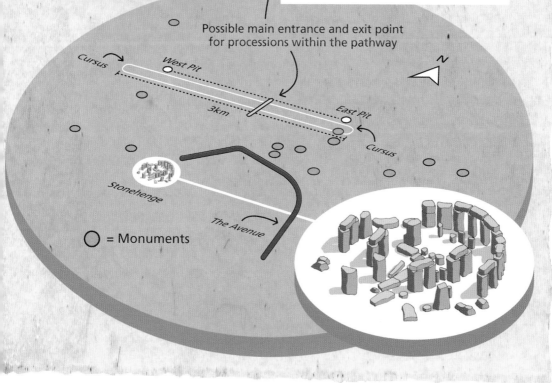

Possible main entrance and exit point for processions within the pathway

Cursus

West Pit

3km

East Pit

Cursus

N

Stonehenge

The Avenue

◯ = Monuments

The Mound of the Hostages is aligned with
the Banqueting Hall

Neolithic religion and megalithic art

Passage tombs were central to Neolithic religion
and were built between approximately
3500 and 3000BC. Artefacts found
in them include stone
basins, deposits of
cremated bone,
pottery, stone
pestle-hammer
pendants, bone
and antler pins (some
mushroom-headed
or poppy-headed),
beads and pendants.
The location of the
megalithic art and
the architecture of the
monument itself were
important to Neolithic ritual.

Megalithic art motifs on
a stone inside the
Mound of the Hostages

Megalithic art

The Boyne Valley in County Meath, which
includes the passage tomb cemeteries of
Newgrange, Knowth and Dowth, contains
the largest collection of megalithic art in
western Europe. Similar examples are found
at Tara in the Mound of the Hostages
passage tomb and at the Iron Age enclosure
of Lismullin. It is likely that the Lismullin
stone was originally a kerbstone from a
passage tomb that was later reused as a
capstone for a medieval souterrain.

Art and religion

There have been controversial studies of
megalithic art that interpret motifs including
grid/lattice patterns, sets of parallel lines,
bright dots, nested curves, zigzag lines and
spirals as expressions of hallucinatory
experiences. These altered states of
consciousness, achieved during religious
rituals, may have been as a result of
ingesting intoxicants, rhythmic dancing,
prayer, fasting, sleep deprivation, isolation,
pain, drumming, near-death experiences,
flickering lights and meditation.

Darkness to light

The Banqueting Hall mirrors the passage
way in the Mound of the Hostages, the
monument with which it is aligned.

The idea of the darkness of the tunnel as a
way into the light of the Otherworld is an idea
found in primitive and modern religions
worldwide. It is the idea of revelation. The
Banqueting Hall can be seen as a tunnel or
vortex into the sacred ritual landscape of Tara.

Shamans have described themselves as
moving between worlds by journeying down a
tunnel or a vortex, sometimes depicted in
megalithic art as a spiral. A large stone with
spirals is situated at the entrance of the
Newgrange passage tomb. The crossing of
thresholds was also very important so the
placing of this stone was strategic.

The Mound of the Hostages

● ● ● ● ● ● ● ● ● ● ● ● ●

The Mound of the Hostages is the oldest monument on the Hill of Tara and is dated to the Neolithic period (3500BC). It consists of a passage with chambers for the reception of the cremated remains of the dead. Like other passage tombs in the Boyne Valley, such as Newgrange and Knowth, its builders had knowledge of astronomy. The sunrise lights up the passageway at Lúnasa (August) and Imbolc (Spring).

The tomb is covered by a mound of earth. It is likely to have got its name from accounts of the exchange of hostages between early medieval kings. There are also stories about the legendary Cormac mac Airt exchanging hostages here.

The passage is divided into three comparments by sill-stones and each one is floored with a single slab. The entrance is flanked by two upright portal stones.

Excavations at the Mound of the Hostages in 1956

The construction of the passage tomb shows a sophisticated knowledge of architecture, engineering, astronomy and art

The Neolithic evidence

Collections of human bone were discovered in the foundation trench of the Mound of the Hostages. Cremated and unburnt bones were found in the chambers. These were the remains of hundreds of individuals. Unburnt human skulls were found buried with cremated bone in the middle part of the tomb; unburnt infant long bones were also found among the cremated adult bones. Clearly, in death, people were not all being treated the same. This may have reflected their perceived status in society. Artefacts recovered included Carrowkeel ware (a pottery associated with passage tombs), stone balls, bone pins and pendants.

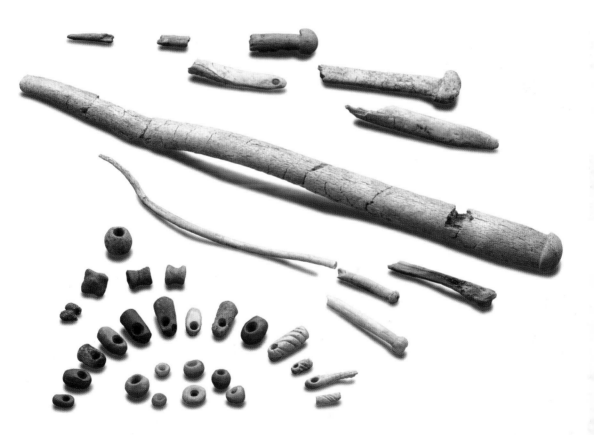

Collection of Neolithic artefacts from the Mound of the Hostages

Bronze Age burials in the Mound of the Hostages

Many of the visible monuments on Tara are barrows dating from the Early to Middle Bronze Age. There were nineteen Early Bronze Age burials inserted in the mound and passage of the Mound of the Hostages. The reuse of the Neolithic passage tomb as a Bronze Age cemetery reflected its continued importance as a sacred site and the importance of being buried with the ancestral dead.

Early Bronze Age inverted collared urn placed over a cremation with a bronze dagger in a pit

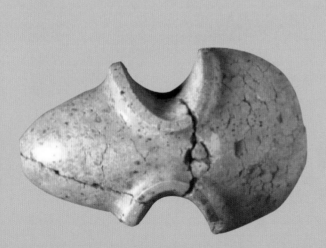

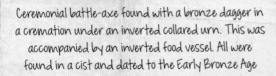

Ceremonial battle-axe found with a bronze dagger in a cremation under an inverted collared urn. This was accompanied by an inverted food vessel. All were found in a cist and dated to the Early Bronze Age

Two Early Bronze Age vase-shaped pottery vessels from the mound. Both were inverted and the larger one enclosed a cremation with a bone pin and some pieces of flint

The Tara 'Boy-King'

In 1955, Seán P. Ó Ríordáin, Professor of Celtic Archaeology at University College Dublin, discovered the remains of a teenager buried in the north western side of the Mound of the Hostages. It was a male adolescent, aged 14 or 15 years. Unlike all the other Early Bronze Age burials, which were cremations on the eastern side of the mound, this was an inhumation.

This individual was buried later than the others and the skeleton was radiocarbon dated to between 1700 and 1600BC. The boy was laid out on his back with his legs flexed to the right and his hands by his sides, with the left hand resting on his pelvis. He was about five feet tall. The burial was in a pit and the skeleton rested on a clay layer that was spread out over a layer of large stones.

The exotic necklace

Unusually this boy was buried with a necklace made of eighteen beads which included materials such as jet, amber, faience and bronze. Jewellery made from jet was very rare in Ireland in the Early Bronze Age as there was no source of good quality jet in the country.

Parallels can be found in Britain. The only significant source of jet there was the area around Whitby in Yorkshire. Most jet beads of this kind have been found in Wessex. The amber beads are also without parallel in Early Bronze Age Ireland. Wessex is also the likely place of origin for them, as raw amber was imported from Denmark to Wessex.

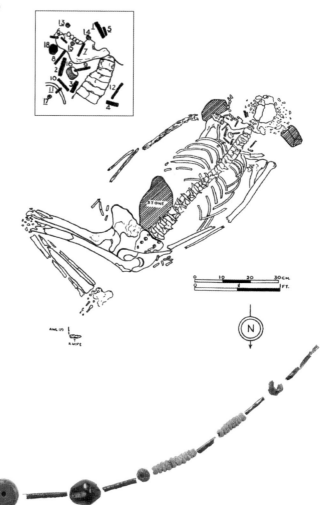

Faience and sheet bronze beads

The Tara faience beads have high arsenic content. Arsenical copper may have been used as a colourant in them. They had not been worn long enough to sustain damage. Faience beads are known from several find-spots in Ireland and are most commonly associated with cordoned urns. Over half the known finds of faience beads in Ireland and Britain combined, however, come from Wessex. The beads of sheet bronze are unique in Ireland but comparisons can also be made with British examples.

The mystery of the necklace

'Composite' necklaces such as this have been found in Wessex, usually in graves with cremated remains. Individuals associated with them are high-status females. The Tara necklace and an example found in Anglesey are exceptions. The only other Irish composite necklace found was with a cordoned urn with a cremated adult female in Altanagh, Co. Tyrone. It is likely that the presence of this type of exotic necklace in the Tara grave demonstrated the boy's high status in society.

Supernatural power-dressing

The necklace represented 'supernatural power-dressing'. It was worn to protect the wearer, a person important enough in Irish society in the Early Bronze Age to be interred in an elite burial place with the ancestors. It was probably an amulet to protect him on his dangerous journey into the afterlife.

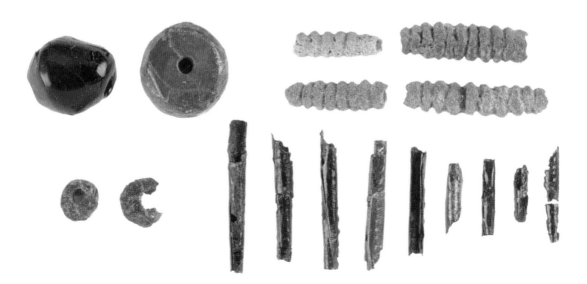

Other grave goods

A small copper-alloy leaf-shaped blade and a fragment of a copper-alloy awl were found close to the boy's feet. Metal awls, used for piercing hide, are known from Early Bronze Age graves in Britain and from a few Early Bronze Age graves in Ireland.

The leaf-shaped blade, thought to be either a knife or a razor, was also found in the grave. Early Bronze Age razors are usually associated with adult males and cordoned urns. It has been suggested that the Tara blade was designed for female use and comparisons have been made with contemporary female graves in Wessex. The fact that the boy was buried with grave goods more appropriate to a female is less important than the fact that he was buried with exotic goods and laid to rest with a different burial rite to the other people buried in the Early Bronze Age cemetery.

An aristocrat or a boy-king?

The grave goods of this boy led archaeologists to pose the following questions:

• Was he an aristocrat or perhaps a young royal?
• Was he from Wessex?
• Had he travelled away from Ireland and brought the necklace back with him?
• Did he add the faience beads on his return?
• Was he a foreigner who had died while visiting Tara?
• Was the necklace imported?

Scientists who examined enamel from a molar tooth found that the boy did not spend his early childhood in the vicinity of Tara nor in the chalklands of Wessex. It is likely that he was originally from Ireland.

The henge

Banqueting Hall

This henge is described as a ditched pit circle. It is not visible in the landscape and was discovered during a geophysical survey. It has a 3m-wide ditch flanked on either side by approximately three hundred regularly spaced post-holes and is comparable in size to Croke Park in Dublin. It may be dated to the Neolithic or Early Bronze Age (c.2500BC). Huge numbers of trees were transported to the site and set upright in pits. This monument was clearly ceremonial in nature. It is similar to timber circles discovered at Brú na Bóinne and Ballynahatty, Co. Antrim. The Rath of the Synods lies close to its centre and the henge is intersected by the Iron Age Ráith na Rí enclosure.

Henges: some interesting facts

- Circular or oval enclosures
- Very large – usually more than 100m in diameter (some as large as 160m)
- Surrounding banks
- Usually a single entrance
- Saucer-shaped interior
- Most do not have internal ditches
- Usually found close to other ritual monuments
- Dating from Neolithic to Iron Age
- Over fifty catalogued in Ireland

Henge/ditched pit circle

Mound of
the Hostages

A reconstruction of the massive henge monument centred at the Rath of the Synods, discovered on the Hill of Tara by archaeologists from The Discovery Programme and NUI Galway using geophysical survey

Ráith na Rí

Ráith na Rí is the largest visible enclosure on Tara and was constructed in the Iron Age c.100BC. It is oval, with a circumference of 1000m, and it has a deep internal ditch and large external bank. These features are generally interpreted as being non-defensive. The ditch was built first, followed by the bank and the internal timber palisade. The palisade concealed what was happening in the interior from the view of those on the outside. The function of the interior was ceremonial.

A deliberate attempt to incorporate pre-existing monuments was made, which suggests that the builders had respect for those monuments and the ancestors they represented. As the architecture of Tara itself was a symbolic representation of the cosmic order, the act of constructing and arranging space in prehistoric times was a sacred activity.

Excavations in progress in 1955 showing a cutting being dug across
the ditch of the Iron Age enclosure Ráith na Rí

View of Ráith na Ríg during excavation, from the north-east

Prehistoric boundaries

The traditional interpretation of monuments like Ráith na Rí was that they functioned as symbolic barriers designed to protect the outside world from Otherworld forces emanating from the large earthen mounds they enclosed. These were thought to be the domain of the ancestors or the *Síd* (Otherworld beings).

Archaeologists have suggested that prehistoric communities believed that artificial boundaries had religious significance. That may be why special deposits were placed in the perimeter ditch of Ráith na Rí. The boundary enclosed a sacred space that was reserved for the performance of rituals.

The burial of human remains or the deliberate placing of objects in a ditch was a means of reinforcing the boundary. Ditches were perceived as special cuts through the life-giving earth. This was the threshold between the earth and the underworld.

Large ceremonial earthworks like Ráith na Rí were also built at other prehiatoric royal sites in Ireland such as Navan Fort, Co. Armagh and Knockaulin, Co. Kildare.

Ráith na Rí: the archaeological evidence

Human remains, animal bones and artefacts
were deposited in the internal ditch of Ráith
na Rí. Human skulls, an infant burial with some
dog bones and burnt and unburnt animal bones
were found during an excavation in 1997.

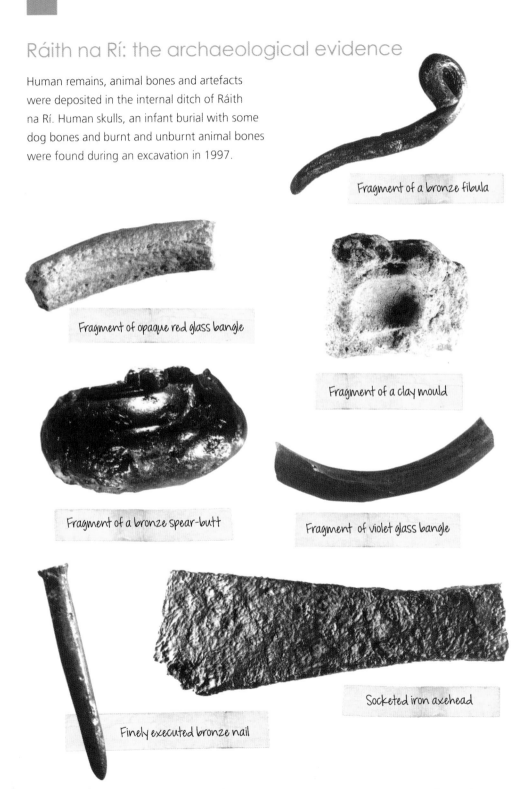

Fragment of a bronze fibula

Fragment of opaque red glass bangle

Fragment of a clay mould

Fragment of a bronze spear-butt

Fragment of violet glass bangle

Socketed iron axehead

Finely executed bronze nail

An infant and a dog

The body of a six-month old child, dated to the first century AD, was deliberately deposited with a dog in the ditch of Ráith na Rí. In late prehistoric Europe dogs had a privileged status. They played an important role in religious practice and many deities and legendary figures had doglike characteristics and names, such as Cú Chulainn (Hound of Culann). Dog bones were often found with human burials. They were not just guardians of the doorway or threshold but were also considered to be guardians against malevolent Otherworldly forces. The burial of a dog with an infant was perhaps an effort to provide a guardian for the child during its journey into the Otherworld.

A human skull

Fourteen cranial and facial bones of an adolescent male were found in Ráith na Rí. In late prehistoric Celtic society the head was held to be the centre of the human soul. Human skulls were considered to have powerful magical attributes.

These human bones were associated with cattle and sheep/goat bones that were deliberately deposited. The animal bones may have been associated with ritual feasting.

Tara workshop

Metalworking activity dating from the Iron Age predated the construction of Ráith na Rí. Evidence for iron and bronze smithing was discovered underneath the external bank. Fragments of crucibles – containers that can withstand very high temperatures used for the production of metal or glass objects – were discovered. Some crucibles with bronze residue, moulds, waste bronze and finished objects were found associated with a metalworking hearth. These represent a rare example of stratified Iron Age bronzeworking in Ireland. A pin and a coil of a bronze fibula brooch dated from the first century BC to the first century AD were also found.

Other interesting artefacts included an iron socketed axe similar to that from Feerwore, Co. Galway. This type of tool is known from La Tène contexts across Europe. Irish smiths were aware of sophisticated methods of metalworking; for example the smith had clearly mastered the technique of forging a right angle. Parallels for this artefact can be found at Beeston Castle in Britain and in the Oppidum Manching in Dunsberg in Germany. Other iron objects found at Tara include nails, staples, brackets, a joiner's dog and a possible awl, used for boring holes in leather or as a gouge for woodworking.

Was glass manufactured at Tara?

Some archaeologist believe that glass splinters found at Tara suggest that glass objects were manufactured at the site. It is likely, however, that the raw glass was imported from Continental Europe. A portion of a purple glass bangle was dated to the first century BC.

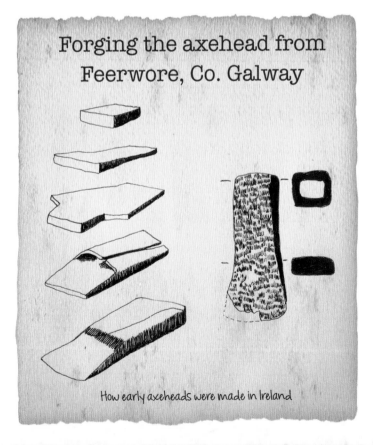

Forging the axehead from Feerwore, Co. Galway

How early axeheads were made in Ireland

A shelter for smiths?

Evidence for a structure, perhaps a shelter for craftsmen, included stake and post-holes and trenches.

The magic of the smith

It is interesting to consider why a metalworking workshop was located in a ritual landscape dominated by funerary monuments and ritual enclosures. Perhaps this was because of the traditional association of the craft of smithing with magical or religious activity. Metal was regarded as having supernatural properties.

The smith-god Goibniu appears in Irish folklore as the *Gobán Saor*, a trickster and many-skilled craftsman. He was a smith, mason, carpenter, shipwright and bridge-builder.

A figure-of-eight

The monuments known as Tech Cormaic and the Forrad were conjoined in a figure-of-eight within Ráith na Rí. There are also similar conjoined earthworks in this formation at Uisneach and Rathcroghan. Tech Cormaic is a ringfort measuring 70m in diameter, with two banks and a ditch. The original entrance is aligned with one of the entrances in Ráith na Rí. There is a low mound with a small hollow in the middle that was possibly a house or the outline of a small barrow. Tech Cormaic was considered in the medieval period to be the royal residence of King Cormac mac Airt.

The Forrad is a flat-topped mound surrounded by a ditch with two outer banks with ditches. It was believed to be the inauguration site for the kings of Tara, regarded as 'world kings'. A small round-topped mound, known as Múr Tea, was one of the barrows that predated and was incorporated into the Forrad monument. Medieval sources describe the burial place of Tea Tephi, an Egyptian princess, as being between the Forrad and Tech Cormaic.

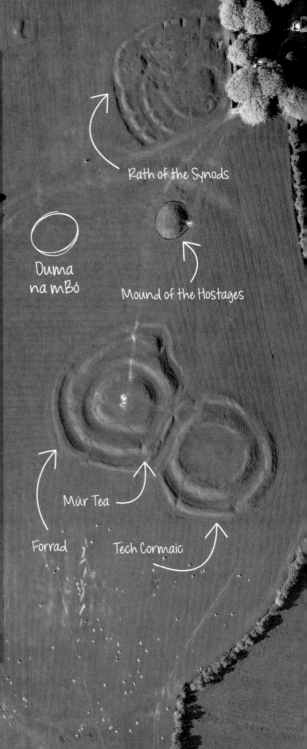

Rath of the Synods

Duma na mBó

Mound of the Hostages

Múr Tea

Forrad

Tech Cormaic

The Lia Fáil

In a medieval survey of Tara, *Dindgnai Temrach* (*The remarkable places of Tara*), the Lia Fáil or stone of destiny was said to have been located to the north of the Mound of the Hostages. It was moved to its current location on top of the Forrad in 1824.

Dindgnai Temrach lists archaeological monuments on Tara such as enclosures and burial mounds and also includes natural features such as streams and springs. The Lia Fáil was described as the stone that roared under the foot of each king that took possession of Ireland. The roar was attributed to the god Lug.

Duma na mBó

Duma na mBó is no longer visible. The nineteenth-century antiquarian, George Petrie, described it as being a mound that was six feet high and forty feet in diameter.

This monument was identified using aerial photography in the 1970s and by geophysical survey carried out by The Discovery Programme in the 1990s.

It is said that a few yards to the west of the coronation mound there formerly stood another mound, which was removed, a few years ago, to make top-dressing for the adjoining pasture land.

A. Dawson, *Tara: a personal visit*, 1901

Rath of the Synods

The Rath of the Synods is a quadrivallate enclosure, which means it has four circular earthen banks with ditches. An unusual feature of this monument are the berms (soil ledges between the ditches and the banks). Evidence for human habitation on the site was dated to the third and fourth centuries AD. The remains of two small rectangular buildings were also found. The Rath of the Synods was reputed to have got its name from the holding of synods there by Irish saints – Patrick in the fifth century, Rúadán in the sixth and Adomnán in the seventh.

A flat cemetery was also discovered that contained seven burials. This included five inhumations and two cremations. Five of the burials contained grave goods but none of these could be clearly dated.

One burial contained a coin, a knife guard, a pin and a disc of copper alloy, an iron pin and possible ear-ring, a bone pin and an animal bone. Animal bones included with burials may be the remains of food offerings for the dead. The mixture of burial rites, including cremation, crouched inhumation and extended inhumation, suggest a date in the late Iron Age (first and second centuries AD).

Burials

Before the construction of the enclosure, the Rath of the Synods was used for burial. The barrow known as the 'King's chair' contained ten burials, five of which were primary cremations. An inhumation in a crouched position was found in the secondary phase of the mound.

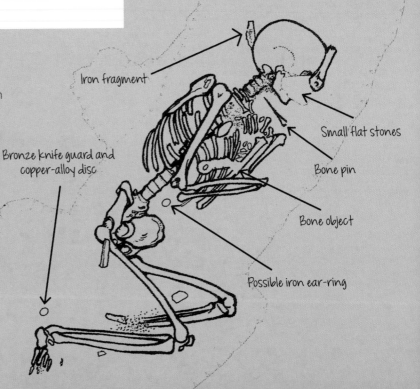

Iron fragment

Bronze knife guard and copper-alloy disc

Small flat stones

Bone pin

Bone object

Possible iron ear-ring

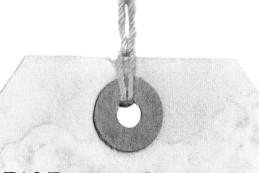

Did Romans live in the Rath of the Synods?

Fifty-five artefacts recovered from the Rath of the Synods have been identified as coming from the Roman world. At least 24% of contexted finds at the Rath of the Synods are Roman including:

- Southern Gaulish Samian ware
- Sherds of flagons (1st–2nd centuries AD)
- Glass vessels (2nd–4th centuries AD)
- Spring from bow brooch
- Dividers
- Mirror fragment
- Lead seal
- Glass inset for ring or brooch
- Glass beads
- Mushroom-headed bronze stud
- Iron barrel padlock (1st–4th century AD)

The seal, dividers, lock, mirror, tools and nails were types used in the Roman world from the first to the fourth century AD. Archaeologists debate whether the occupants of the site were a native affluent elite importing exotic material or an immigrant domestic group using standard Roman items. Roman material has also been found at Lambay Island and Drumanagh, both in County Dublin, Stoneyford, Co. Kilkenny and Newgrange, Co. Meath. In Bray, Co. Wicklow, coins of Trajan (97–117) and Hadrian (117–138) were found with people buried according to Roman custom.

It was not necessary for the Romans to invade Ireland to have cultural influence. In the first to fourth centuries AD the Romans were influential across Europe through conquest, trade and travel.

Tara was a powerful place and it is possible that people from the Roman world travelled to meet with kings. Irishmen also served in the Roman army and may have returned to Ireland with Roman objects.

Roman pottery

Twenty-four potsherds were recovered from the Rath of the Synods. These come from a minimum of eight vessels. All are Samian ware, a variety of red-gloss pottery made mainly in Gaul (now Belgium and France) and Germany and exported to Britain from the mid-first to the mid-third century AD.

This was not typical of Roman pottery assemblages as none of the common Romano-British greywares or black burnished wares were found at Tara.

Sherds of Roman pottery found at the Rath of the Synods

MOURNI

Ceremonial feasting

Most of the pots from Tara are finewares and five are drinking vessels. It is possible that the Tara pottery represents the remains of funerary meals or ceremonial feasting.

An example of a Roman Samian ware bowl

DECEASED

Glass

Glass found at the Rath of the Synods consisted mainly of bowls and beakers used for drinking. One sherd, a mold-blown bowl dating from the second to the third century AD, was transparent and of the highest quality Roman table glass.

A cone beaker, like those found in fourth century contexts throughout western Europe, contained a wheel-engraved decoration. This type of Roman tableware indicated the presence of high-quality imports to Tara. Vessels dating from the second to fourth centuries were found. The use of imported glass drinking vessels on high-status and ceremonial sites continued beyond this period.

Trades and manufacturing

There was evidence for manufacturing and thirty tools including awls, blades, chisels, points, staples and rubbing stones. Nails made in a Roman manner, and some larger ones of the type used in the building of Roman forts, were also recovered.

An example of a Roman glass bowl

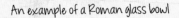

Collection of small finds from the Rath of the Synods

Evidence for slaves

A barrel padlock, similar to the type found on Romano-British sites, was dated to the late second century. Barrel padlocks were used to restrain humans and examples have been found with slave-chains on sites in Europe.

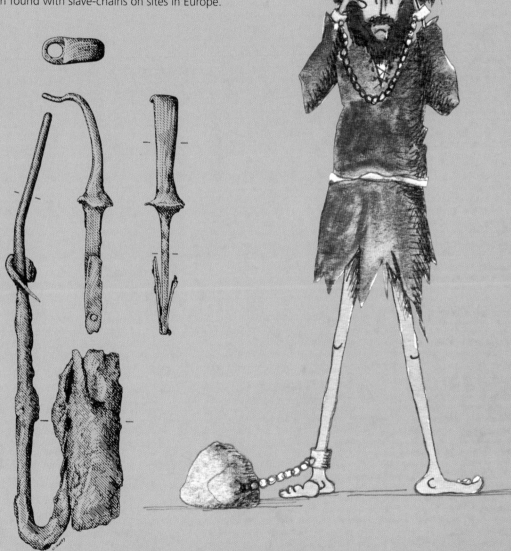

Roman barrel padlock and bolt found in the Rath of the Synods

No restraining chain was found at Tara. A Romano-British key of a type that would have unlocked the Tara padlock was found at the royal site of Uisneach, Co. Westmeath.

Ráith Gráinne & the Sloping Trenches

Ráith Gráinne, like the Sloping Trenches (Clóenfherta), is one of the largest ring-barrows on the Hill of Tara and all three incorporate earlier monuments. It is likely to have been a place of assembly.

Lidar model of Ráith Grainne

Fionn mac Cumaill acquired his remarkable wisdom by tasting the Salmon of Knowledge that was caught in the River Boyne

Gráinne

Gráinne, daughter of the legendary king Cormac mac Airt, had her wedding feast with Fionn mac Cumaill, leader of the Fianna, in the Banqueting Hall. It was during this feast that she made the decision that she would prefer to marry one of his followers, Diarmuid Ó Duibhne. Gráinne eloped with Diarmuid and they were chased across Ireland by Fionn and his men. Many archaeological monuments were named to commemorate them. Diarmuid was eventually killed by a wild boar.

Sloping Trenches

The monuments known as the Northern and Southern Clóenfherta (Sloping Trenches) are two of the largest Bronze Age ring-barrows on the Hill of Tara. There are also three mounds visible between the Northern and Southern Clóenfherta – these are possible bowl barrows.

King Lugaid mac Con's false judgement

According to legend, King Lugaid mac Con made a false judgement that led to the collapse of the Northern Clóenfherta. He was subsequently advised by his druids to leave Tara.

Lismullin

In prehistoric times people living in the hinterland of the ritual landscape of Tara probably moved to different monuments for particular activities. In this sacred landscape monuments were designated for specific use such as assembly, defence, ritual procession, inauguration of kings, astronomical events and power points where the priest-kings accessed the Otherworld.

The Iron Age temple discovered in the valley below Tara at Lismullin was a ritual site and could be viewed from the Rath of the Synods. Perhaps the prehistoric priest-king of Tara was king of all he surveyed in the landscape, including Lismullin, from the apex of the Hill of Tara?

The archaeological excavation in progress at Lismullin

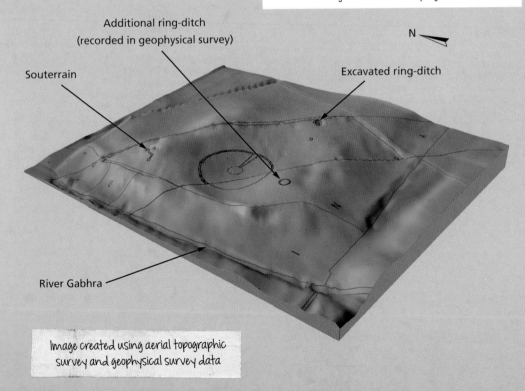

Additional ring-ditch (recorded in geophysical survey)

Souterrain

Excavated ring-ditch

N

River Gabhra

Image created using aerial topographic survey and geophysical survey data

Lismullin: astronomy and power

The prehistoric builders showed knowledge of astronomy, mathematics and engineering in the construction of the Lismullin ceremonial monument in the Middle Iron Age. There was a single post-hole marking the geometric centre. This was probably used in setting out the monument and also served as a symbolic centre point – perhaps an *axis mundi* – the 'centre of the world'.

The monument consisted of 590 posts in total. It has been suggested that these were substituted for trees that were important in late prehistoric religion. These posts were used to construct a large enclosure with two concentric rings.

The outer ring measured 80m in diameter. A small inner enclosure contained a single ring of posts and measured 16m in diameter. It had no formal entrance. In the outer enclosure an entrance was constructed of four substantial upright posts.

An avenue of upright stakes linked the large enclosure to the inner enclosure. There was an elongated pit discovered just inside the entrance area at Lismullin. Large quantities of charcoal, dating from 400 to 200BC, were found. Hazelnut shells, burnt and unburnt animal bones including pig, horse and sheep/goat were also recovered. These may have been food offerings.

A similar sanctuary

Lismullin can be broadly compared to the Belgic sanctuaries found in northern France, such as the sub-rectangular earthwork enclosure at Gournay-sur-Aronde. This was built in the fourth century BC. It consisted of successive timber built temples. At the entrance was a large pit; entry could be gained via a footbridge over this pit.

A drawing of the Belgic sanctuary, Gournay-sur-Aronde, Northern France

Worshipping the cosmos

The role of astronomy in prehistoric religious practice was important. The avenue at Lismullin was aligned on the Pleiades, the star cluster nearest to Earth. It was prominent in the sky and visible to the naked eye for about three months from the end of harvest to the onset of winter. This star cluster is also known as the Seven Sisters and in Greek mythology these were the daughters of Atlas.

With the development of agriculture the movements of the sun became very important. It is possible that homage to the sun was reflected in the architecture of Lismullin with its circular layout.

While it is impossible to gauge the ordinary prehistoric person's perception of the cosmos, it is likely that they had a sense of awe and mystery while watching astronomical events and associated ceremonies. The ceremonies probably took place at night when the Pleiades alignment was visible.

What happened at Lismullin?

Picture the scene: the community watching the ceremonies from the ridge of high ground overlooking the enclosure. The king and his entourage lead the ceremony through the entrance, into the avenue, over the elongated pit, deposit a food offering to the gods into the pit on the ritual routeway and continue into the inner sanctuary where the ritual lighting of fires was enacted. Archaeological evidence was found for the lighting of fires in the inner enclosure.

An Irish sky-burial

The discovery of a building with four timber uprights, set in post-pits and packed with stones, was intriguing. As it measured only 3m² it was too small an area for a house. It probably supported a wooden platform.

It is likely that it was used for excarnation; this involved the placing of a dismembered human body on a platform or altar for birds to eat.

A shrine

A building dating to the Late Bronze Age (8th–6th century BC) was constructed of numerous small wooden posts. It was 12m² and had bowed walls with rounded corners. The entrance consisted of two parallel lines of post-holes. All the post-holes contained burnt bone.

No domestic refuse or evidence for a hearth in the interior were found. It is likely that it was temple or a shrine.

There was evidence for large quantities of *maloideae* (small flowering trees or shrubs), probably used for ornamental purposes.

Assembly and defence

Rath Maeve

Rath Maeve is a very large circular enclosure half a mile south of the Hill of Tara. It is possible it was used for the purpose of assembly. According to legend Maeve Lethderg of Tara organized the building of her own fort during a period when she briefly held the kingship of Tara. This was during the time that Cormac mac Airt was expelled from Tara for fourteen months. In the *Book of Leinster* it was claimed that Maeve would not tolerate a king at Tara who did not take her as a wife.

A BRONZE AGE UNION REP

Cormac mac Airt could not become king of Tara until he slept with Maeve. She was also wife of others in Cormac's line as well as wife of a king of Leinster. A tract in the *Book of Lecan* says that she slept with nine kings of Ireland but it does not name them.

Hill of Tara

Rath Maeve

Defending Tara

Three large enclosures in prominent positions encircle the Hill of Tara, including Ringlestown Rath to the south-west, Rathmiles to the north and Rath Lugh to the north-east. The position of these enclosures and their elevations in relation to the surrounding landscape suggests their use as a defence. They guarded the access to the valley and the Hill of Tara.

They were probably built in the final centuries BC and the early centuries AD and are somewhat similar to hillforts in construction, despite being smaller in scale. They were built to be visible in the landscape from the Hill of Tara and they may also have been used as assembly areas.

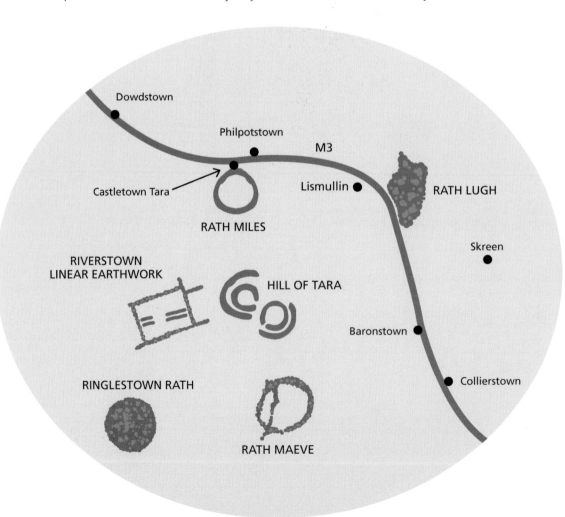

Cú Chulainn at Ringlestown Rath

When Cú Chulainn was a boy he left Navan Fort in his chariot to travel to the dwelling place of Nechtan Scéne, believed to have been located at Ringlestown Rath. The sons of Nechtan Scéne had boasted that they had killed as many Ulstermen as there were living in the province of Ulster. When he got there he stopped at a pillar-stone that had an iron collar around it and ogham writing on it which said that any man who came bearing arms should challenge a man from the fort before he left. Cú Chulainn lifted the pillar-stone and threw it into water nearby. Then he spread out the covering of his chariot on the grass and went to sleep. Foil, one of the sons of Nechtan

Scéne, arrived. He questioned Cú Chulainn about his ability to fight. Neither the point of a spear nor the edge of a sword could harm Foil, so Cú Chulainn fought him using his iron ball. He hurled it at Foil's head and it went through Foil's forehead, along with his brains. Then Cú Chulainn cut off his head.

Then the second son of Nechtan Scéne, Tuachel, arrived. Tuachel had to be killed by the first blow or he could not be killed at all. Cú Chulainn used King Conchobar mac Neasa's great sword to kill Tuathel and also cut off his head. Then Fainnle, the youngest son of Nechtan, came out. Fainnle challenged Cú Chulainn to fight in the water. Fainnle could travel across water with the swiftness of a swallow. Cú Chulainn wrestled with him and cut Fainnle's head off with Conchobar's sword. He took the three heads of the sons of Nechtan Scéne as trophies back to Navan Fort. Cú Chulainn's arm and head are reputed to be buried at Tara.

Cú Chulainn, the mythical warrior and hero of *Táin Bó Cúailnge* (*The Cattle Raid of Cooley*)

Navan Fort, Co. Armagh

Comparable royal sites

Navan Fort

The royal site of Navan Fort is located outside Armagh City. The main circular enclosure (250m in approx. diameter) is dated to the Iron Age. It has a ditch on the inside and a bank on the outside like Ráith na Rí. This means that this monument was used for ritual and not defensive purposes. Inside the enclosure a ring-barrow and a mound are visible. It is also part of a wider archaeological landscape.

Other monuments in this ritual complex include possible passage tombs, ring-ditches, a Late Bronze Age hillfort known as Haughey's Fort, an artificial ritual pool and natural features such as lakes and bogs. This site was first used in the Neolithic period; evidence for this includes flint tools and sherds of pottery dating from c.4000 to c.2500BC.

Iron Age temple

In 95BC, a structure was built in the shape of a round house consisting of four concentric rings of posts surrounding a central oak trunk. The floor was covered with stones which were set in radial segments. This structure was intentionally burnt down before being covered with a mound of earth and turf.

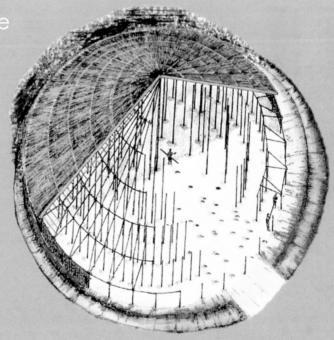

Round house ritual structure: the centre of the world at Navan Fort

Rathcroghan

The royal site of Rathcroghan, located near Tulsk, Co. Roscommon, consists of over sixty monuments. These include settlement enclosures, barrows, ring-ditches and linear earthworks. Rathcroghan mound is circular and flat topped. It was originally revetted with a timber palisade and surrounded by a ditched enclosure. There is evidence for entrance avenues similar to those in Navan Fort and Knockaulin.

The cave of the cats: entrance to the Otherworld?

This site is a souterrain underneath an old road leading into a limestone cave. In tradition it is the entrance to the Otherworld. In the stories mythological creatures emerged from this cave. It may have got its name from 'Bricriu's Feast', a story in which the Ulster champions fought large wild cats. Two of the stones used to build the souterrains contain ogham inscriptions: one refers to Fráech, son of Medb.

The cave of the cats (Oweynagat)

Uisneach: the 'navel' of Ireland

This ceremonial site, near Mullingar, Co. Westmeath, includes a megalithic tomb, ring-ditches, standing-stones, ringforts, mounds and ring-barrows. A prominent hilltop enclosure with a mound at its centre is similar to features at Tara (Ráith na Rí), Knockaulin and Navan Fort.

Figure-of-eight

There was evidence for two conjoined enclosures in the same figure-of-eight form found at other royal sites. These were dated to the early medieval period and each contained a house and a souterrain. These structures had been built on an earlier Iron Age ditched enclosure. Human remains were found in the ditch and internal area of this enclosure. There was evidence for feasting, animal sacrifice and the lighting of fires. The tradition of lighting a fire on the Hill of Uisneach is still continued to this day at the festival of Beltaine (May Day).

Roman material

Roman material including a barrel padlock key and a coin of the emperor Magnentius (dating to the mid-fourth century AD) were recovered. Roman material was also found at Tara and Knockaulin.

The Cat Stone

The Cat Stone at Uisneach is a natural stone situated in the centre of an earthen enclosure. The fact that this enclosure surrounded the Cat Stone marked the latter as a monument of significance. It was described by the Welsh clergyman and historian, Gerald of Wales (c.1146–1223), as *umbilicus Hibernie*, the 'navel of Ireland'.

The Cat Stone at Uisneach: the navel of Ireland

Knockaulin

Knockaulin is a royal site in County Kildare. According to tradition, the kings of Leinster were inaugurated there. It is situated in a wider archaeological landscape consisting of one hundred and eighty monuments including barrows, enclosures, ring-ditches and linear earthworks. In the large oval earthwork enclosure there is an internal ditch, mound and an ancient roadway. The internal ditch suggests that the enclosure was used for ceremonial purposes. While there was evidence for use of the site in the Neolithic period, most of the activity took place in the Iron Age.

Figure-of-eight

A series of Iron Age timber structures were discovered during excavation. One of these had a figure-of-eight layout. Artefacts recovered included an iron sword, an iron spearhead, iron needles, fragments of a bronze fibula and some glass beads.

Ceremonial feasting

Large quantities of bones from sheep, pigs, cows, deer and horses were found, which may indicate that some ceremonial feasting took place.

3: Tara in medieval times

Niall of the Nine Hostages: ancestor of historical kings of Tara?

Niall of the Nine Hostages is one of the most famous kings of Tara and one of the most intriguing figures associated with the site. There are mythological tales in which he has the starringrole; he is considered to be the ancestor of historical kings of Tara. Modern scientists have carried out studies in an effort to establish if there is a scientific basis for his existence.

Niall and the sovereignty goddess

In the story *The adventures of the sons of Eochaid Muigmedón*, Niall of the Nine Hostages mated with the goddess of sovereignty. She appeared to him as an ugly hag but was transformed into a beautiful woman because Niall was the rightful king of Tara. Niall of the Nine Hostages was described in the seventh-century *Life of Patrick* by Muirchú maccu Machtheni as 'the one from whom was descended the royal stock of almost the entire island'. Niall's son, Lóegaire, was described as 'emperor of the barbarians ruling in Tara, which was the capital of the Irish'.

Genetic imprint

A team of geneticists at Trinity College Dublin carried out research on the possible descendants of Niall of the Nine Hostages by studying the genetic signature of males with surnames linked to Niall. They revealed that it seemed likely that the number of descendants worldwide was in the region of two to three million males. They published their paper in *The American Journal of Human Genetics* in 2006. They reached the conclusion that:

'Figures such as Niall of the Nine Hostages reside at the cusp of mythology and history, but our results do seem to confirm the existence of a single early medieval progenitor to the most powerful and enduring Irish dynasty'.

However, the historical existence of Niall of the Nine Hostages was not proven by the Trinity study.

Archaeological evidence

Other important scientific studies such as the geophysical survey of Niall's reputed burial place, Faughan Hill, Co. Meath, were also carried out. This site, situated in the catchment zone of Tara, was identified as the ancient site of Ocha. Ocha was an important regional centre in the early centuries AD and the reputed site of the battle that took place in 482 between Niall's descendants and other rival claimants to the kingship of Tara.

'Many Irishmen boast descent from kings'.
F.J. Byrne, Irish kings and high kings

Faughan Hill: the reputed burial place of Niall of the Nine Hostages

Faughan Hill consists of large hilltop enclosures and ring-ditches.The presence of these monuments suggest that it was a place of assembly, ceremony and burial in prehistory. Sites nearby, including Tlachtga (the Hill of Ward), the Hill of Lloyd and Teltown, had similar functions. Faughan Hill was used over a long period of time. High-status Roman objects found in the vicinity suggest it was used in the late Iron Age. There was also an early Christian church, Domnach Pátraic, nearby. All of these sites, including Tara, were in the kingdom of Brega.

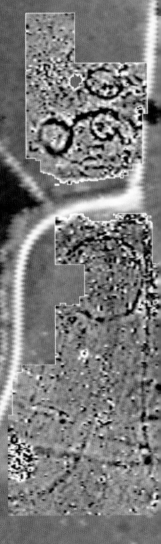

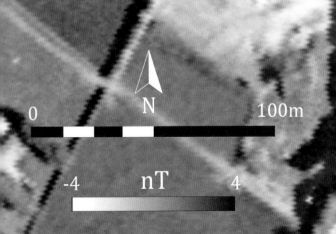

N

0 100m

-4 nT 4

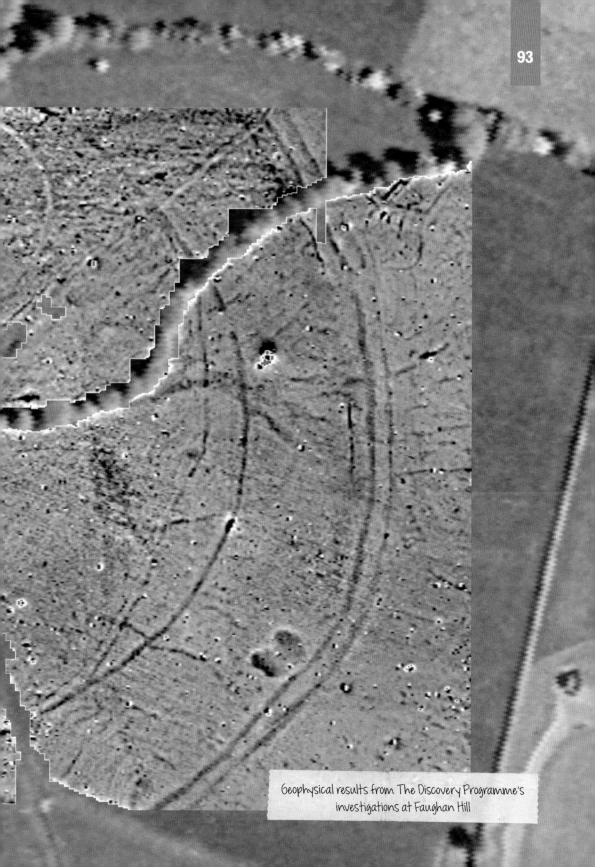

Geophysical results from The Discovery Programme's
investigations at Faughan Hill

Niall of the Nine Hostages: family tree

This is the family tree of Niall of the Nine Hostages. His ancestors include the legendary kings of Tara, Conn of the Hundred Battles and Cormac mac Airt. His descendants include historic kings of Tara of the Uí Néill dynasty.

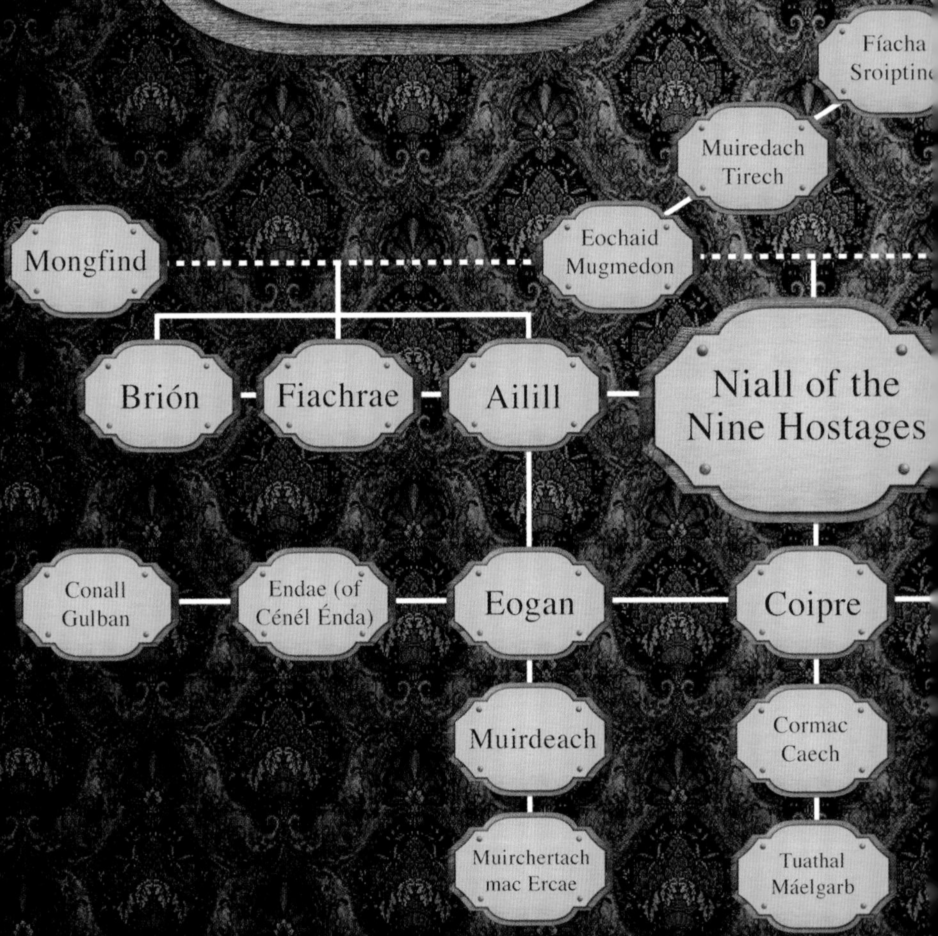

Fíacha Sroiptine

Muiredach Tirech

Eochaid Mugmedon

Mongfind

Brión — Fiachrae — Ailill — Niall of the Nine Hostages

Conall Gulban — Endae (of Cénél Énda) — Eogan — Coipre

Muirdeach

Cormac Caech

Muirchertach mac Ercae

Tuathal Máelgarb

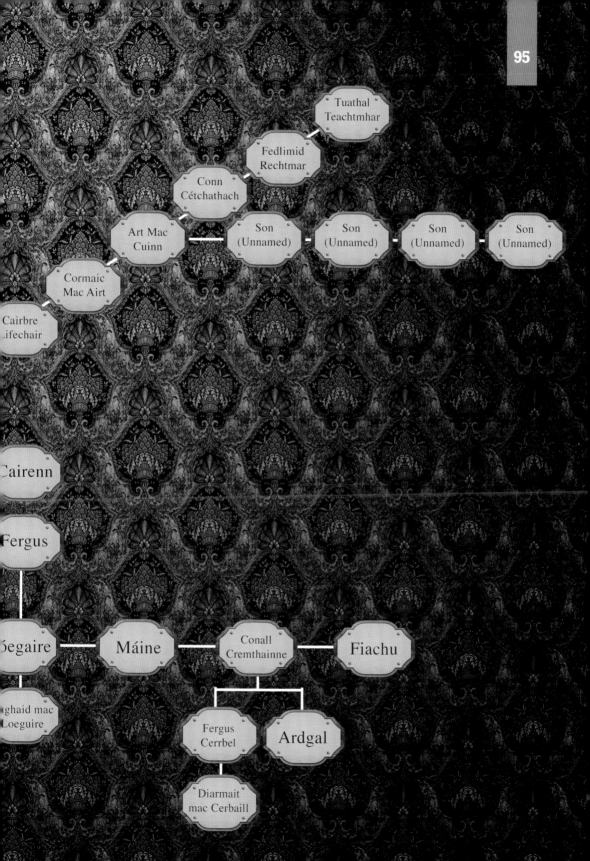

Tuathal Teachtmhar

Fedlimid Rechtmar

Conn Cétchathach

Art Mac Cuinn — Son (Unnamed) — Son (Unnamed) — Son (Unnamed) — Son (Unnamed)

Cormaic Mac Airt

Cairbre Lifechair

Cairenn

Fergus

Lóegaire — Máine — Conall Cremthainne — Fiachu

ghaid mac Loeguire

Fergus Cerrbel — Ardgal

Diarmait mac Cerbaill

The Uí Néill dynasty

Tara, as an important royal site in medieval Ireland,
was closely associated with the Uí Néill dynasty
which was said to be descended from Niall of the
Nine Hostages. He was believed to have lived some time
around the middle of the fifth century AD. By the end
of the fifth century the north-eastern Ulaid
and south-eastern Laigen had lost the
kingship of Tara to the Uí Néill.

Northern Uí Néill

Ulaid

Airgialla

Bréifne

Connacht
Connachta

Southern Uí Néill

Dublin

Leinster
Laigen

Limerick

Osraige

Munster
Mumu

Wexford

Waterford

Cork

While the king of Tara was a very powerful ruler he rarely succeeded in holding all of the island subject to him. The medieval idea of the political high kingship of Tara was promoted to further the political interests of the Uí Néill, who dominated Ireland until the eleventh century. The provinces of Ireland including Mumu (Munster), Connacht, Laigen (Leinster), Mide and Ulaid were ruled by provincial kings. The king of Tara did not always act as an over-king of the other provincial kings. He was probably always the most powerful king in the north but rarely had power over Munster. It was not until the mid-tenth century that the 'king of Tara' was widely and consistently referred to as 'king of Ireland'. The Uí Néill dynasty itself was divided into two main branches, northern and southern.

Tara and Christianity

St Patrick

In the seventh-century life of St Patrick written by Muirchú moccu Mactheni, there is a story about the saint lighting the Paschal fire on the Hill of Slane (Co. Meath) to celebrate the Christian feast of Easter in opposition to the fire lit by the pagan king Lóegaire on Tara to celebrate the existing traditional festival of Beltaine (May Day).

Lóegaire, son of Niall of the Nine Hostages, had summoned the kings, nobles, druids, and craftsmen to Tara for the occasion. As was the custom, it was announced that anyone who lit a fire on that night before the king of Tara would be put to death. St Patrick ignored this threat. This was a challenge to Lóegaire as king and to the institution of the kingship of Tara. The text written by Muirchú shows that the Christian clergy were worried about the power of the druids as late as the seventh century. Patrick, according to some versions of the story, succeeded in converting Lóegaire and his druids to Christianity.

Lá Fhéile Pádraig   ÉIRE 65c

2006

Seán Keating | St. Patrick Lights the Paschal Fire at Slane

'St Patrick's Day, 2006' stamp depicting St Patrick lighting the paschal fire at Slane

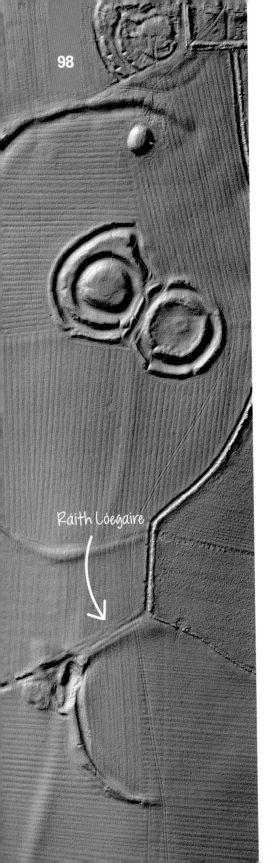

Ráith Lóegaire

Kingship and Christianity

Tara retained its significance even after the introduction of Christianity. However, the pre-Christian model of kingship was changed even though the monuments themselves were not christianized. It was now essential that kingship be imbued with the values of Christianity.

The universal concept of kingship was key to a well-ordered society and these positive ideals could be retained in a Christian society. Stories about kings of Tara changed to reflect how Christian ideas had remoulded the kingship. For example, King Feargal mac Maíle Dúin had two sons and tested both to see who would succeed him. The older son engaged in a night of debauchery. The younger spent it in thanks-giving to God and singing praises to the Lord. The father prophesied that his younger son would reign in the future and that his descendants would become famous and royal.

Standing burial

According to tradition the body of Lóegaire was interred in a standing position with his shield in the external rampart of Tara, facing south, as if he were fighting against his enemies, the Laigen (Leinstermen). Warriors in some ancient societies, such as the Anglo-Saxons, were buried standing up as a mark of respect.

Conversion of King Lóegaire's daughters

Lóegaire's daughters, Eithne and Fedelm, together with their druid Máel, were said to have been converted by St Patrick at the royal site of Rathcroghan and interred there.

Stories like this reflect the tensions between retaining the traditions of the old pagan religion and the gradual introduction of the new religion of Christianity and the power struggles this entailed.

Window depicting Eithne and Fedelm, the daughters of the king of Tara, Lóegaire mac Néill, by Harry Clarke

Did St Patrick make Tara crooked?

In the *Senchas Már*, a legal text in the Irish language probably originally compiled in the seventh century, there is a poem about how St Patrick caused monuments on Tara to become crooked. In it, Lóegaire encouraged the killing of Patrick's charioteer to see if the saint would forgive the deed. His own brother, also his hostage, agreed to carry out the killing provided Lóegaire released him. He took up a spear and duly killed the charioteer.

St Patrick was enraged and lifted up his arms to God. With this there was an earthquake and darkness fell and the gates of Hell were opened. Tara was twisted around and made crooked. This resulted in the formation of the Sloping Trenches.

There are medieval tales of the origins of the Sloping Trenches

This effort to explain the presence of these Bronze Age barrows on the Hill of Tara in a Christian context reflects the fact that Irish society was, by then, a Christian one. However, St Patrick does not mention Tara in his own writings.

Adomnán's Cross

Abbot Adomnán of Iona (679–704) was
one of the most important figures in the
seventh-century Irish church. From the
foundation of Iona by Columba (about
565) to the death of Adomnán, all nine
abbots were of the Uí Néill kin. The last
quarter of the seventh century was
especially characterized by close
cooperation between abbot and kings of
both branches of the Uí Néill. Around
700 the power of the clergy was
increasing and Adomnán was in favour
of the idea that an abbot could conse-
crate a king. This was an attempt to
Christianize sacral kingship.

A limestone pillar in the churchyard at
Tara is called Adomnán's Cross. There
is a small figure carved on the cross in
relief which has been identified as a
late medieval Sheela-na-gig.

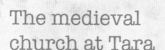

The medieval church at Tara

The present church at Tara stands alongside the site of an earlier medieval church that was associated with the Knights Hospitallers of St John of Kilmainham in County Dublin. The Hospitallers' possessions, including the church at Tara, were confirmed to them by Pope Innocent III in 1212. The church was said to be a functioning parish church until the sixteenth century, after which it fell into disrepair. In 1622 the Protestant Bishop of Dublin, James Ussher, visited Tara and noted that the church and chancel were in ruins. The modern Church of Ireland church was built on this site in 1822.

Feis Temro

Diarmait mac Cerbaill, of the southern Uí Néill dynasty (said to be the great grandson of Niall of the Nine Hostages), was King of Tara between 544 and 565. He was reputed to have been the last king of Tara to celebrate *Feis Temro*, an ancient ritual feast, in 560. *Feis Temro* confirmed the sacral kingship, the word *feis* referring to the mating of the sacral king with the sovereignty goddess. This ritual expressed the idea of the fertility of the land as being essential to a successful kingship. This feast was also associated with the festival of Samhain (modern Halloween). The word *feis* is often mentioned in medieval Irish literature. Even outsiders like Gerald of Wales describe the inauguration of the Cenél Conaill king in terms of a *feis*. This description is sometimes seen as propaganda to portray the Irish as pagan and barbaric.

Inauguration of a medieval king

The ceremonial aspects of the inauguration of a king included:

· The granting of the rod of sovereignty

· A procession symbolizing the regions under the king's rule

· The holding of a horse race

· The singing of praise poetry

· The drinking of royal ale from a special drinking horn

Battling over Tara: political power struggles

Ireland c. 700

The kingdom of Brega was a region of fertile land defined by the area between the River Dee, Co. Louth and the River Liffey, Co. Dublin. This was the most important region in medieval Ireland.

As it was defined by the sea on the eastern side, it was a point of entry into Ireland at the Boyne Estuary. There were many ceremonial centres in the region of Brega, including the prehistoric ritual landscapes of Tara, Newgrange, Knowth and Dowth. In order to realize their political ambitions, provincial kings needed to assert their authority over the kingdom of Brega.

The cursing of Tara: St Rúadán

In a medieval tale St Rúadán of Lorrha was described as having cursed Diarmait mac Cerbaill, which led to the abandonment of Tara. This was in response to Diarmait violating the sanctuary of St Rúadán at his monastery in Rahan. Twelve saints assembled at Tara to curse Diarmait and Tara. Rúadán was reputed to have said 'May Temair be deserted,' and 'may there not be a dwelling place upon her forever'. This tale may reflect the church's dislike of Tara and its fear of its continuing potency.

Battle of Tara, 980

When the Vikings were well established in Dublin, their king Amlaíb Cuarán attempted to stamp his authority over the kingdom of Brega. He was stopped at the Battle of Tara in 980 by Máel Sechlainn mac Domnaill, king of Tara and arch-rival of the king of Munster, Brian Ború. The northern and southern borders of Brega were noted battlegrounds.

The *Dindshenchas* of Tara

The medieval text, the *Dindshenchas,* or *Lore of places*, was a particularly rich mythological and topographical source. It is preserved in prose and metrical versions in manuscripts such as the twelfth-century *Book of Leinster* and the fourteenth-century *Book of Ballymote*. It explains how numerous places got their names and has been described as the mythical geography of the country.

The literary corpus includes about one hundred and seventy-six poems and a number of prose commentaries and tales. The *Dindshenchas* of Tara includes five poems and two prose extracts. Cuán Ua Lothchan, Ireland's chief poet and historian, wrote some of the poems. He linked monuments on the Hill of Tara to ancestral kings and queens.

King Máel Sechlainn and the *Dindshenchas*

Parts of the *Dindshenchas* of Tara was compiled in order to enhance the political claims of the southern Uí Néill, particularly that of Máel Sechlainn mac Domnaill, king of Tara, who died in 1022 after ruling for forty-three years.

In prehistory the land had been claimed by building prominent and important monuments as statements of power. A return to the authority of the monuments to reconnect with powerful forces of the past was important to the Uí Néill dynasty. In medieval times this power, stemming from history, was achieved through the written word. The name and landscape of Tara became a powerful political symbol for Máel Sechlainn who was involved in ongoing political power struggles with the northern Uí Néill, the Vikings and Brian Ború.

The importance of prehistoric burial places

In the ninth-century text, *The Martyrology of Óengus*, the ruined, abandoned pre-Christian sites of power including Tara, Rathcroghan and Navan Fort were contrasted with the flourishing ecclesiastical centres of Clonmacnoise and Armagh. But the burial places of the ancestors, as physical places in the landscape, retained their sacred nature and were still an expression of power in medieval times. They symbolized the transference of power from the ancestors to the medieval kings, legitimizing their claims to the lands in the process.

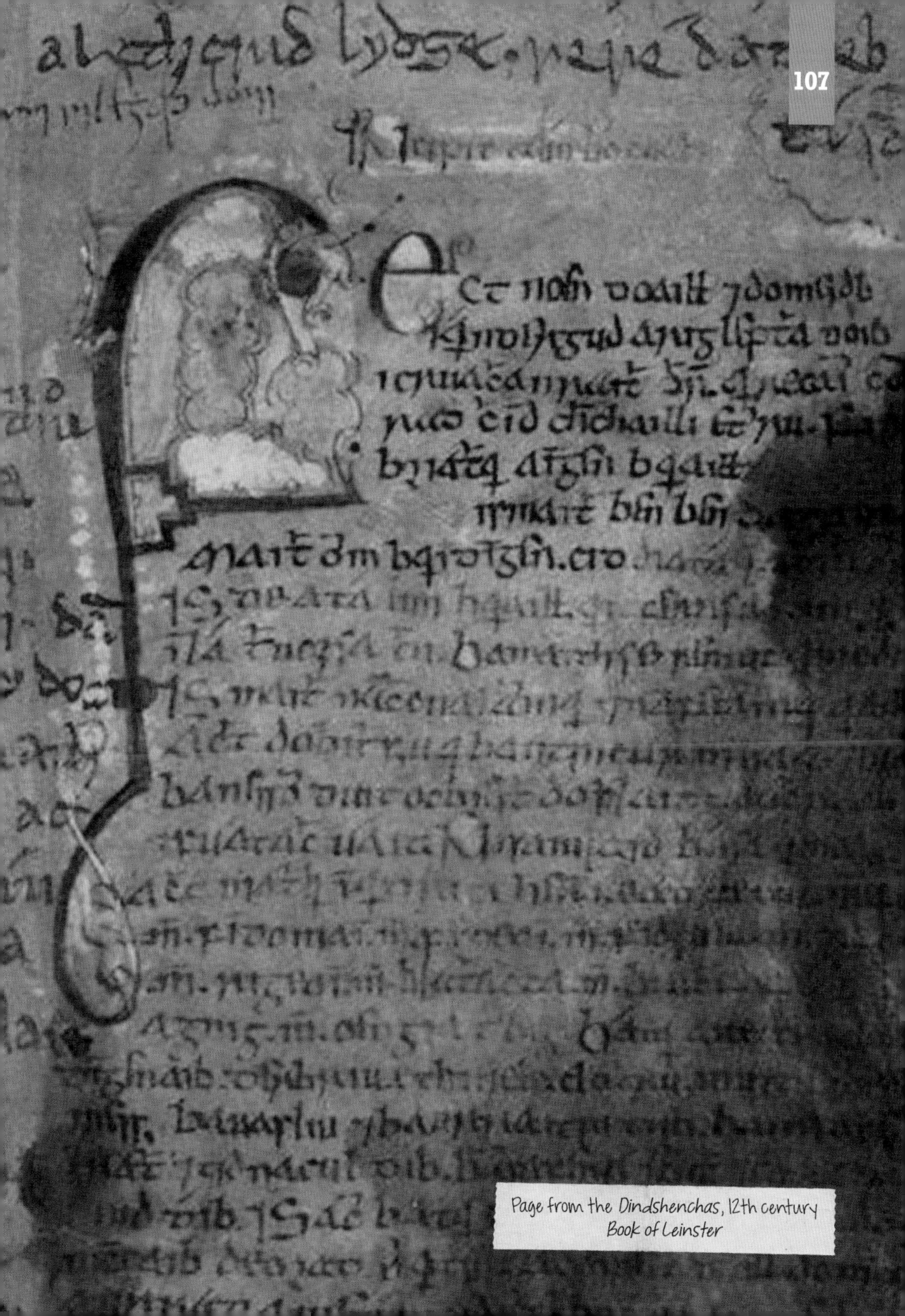

Page from the *Dindshenchas*, 12th century Book of Leinster

Brian Ború and the kingship of Ireland

Brian Ború, king of Munster, challenged the dominance of the Uí Néill and their hold on the kingship of Tara. He began a series of campaigns to assert his authority over all of Ireland. In 977 Vikings helped him to kill the king of Limerick and his two sons in the monastery of Scattery Island. This act brought Limerick under his control. He became king of Cashel in 978 and over-king of Munster. This put him in a strong position to pursue his goal of attaining the kingship of Ireland. He allied himself with Vikings in Waterford and in the Isle of Man against the Vikings of Dublin. According to the Annals of Inisfallen (996) Brian Ború fortified Cashel as part of his defence of Munster against Máel Sechlainn mac Domnaill, king of Tara.

By 1014, when the Battle of Clontarf took place, members of Viking and Irish dynasties had a history of intermarriage. This facilitated cultural exchange, alliances and trade that crossed political boundaries. Some Vikings had converted to Christianity and gave their support to some churches while raiding the churches associated with their enemies. At Clontarf Brian Ború's army emerged victorious despite the fact that he was killed. He is generally depicted as a pious Irish Christian king who was praying in his tent when he was attacked and killed by a vengeful pagan Viking. He was in reality a warlord who had at least four wives and a few concubines.

Gormlaith and all her kings

One of Brian Ború's wives was Queen Gormlaith. In the eleventh-century *War of the Irish with the foreigners,* Gormlaith is described as inciting her brother Máelmórda to rebel against her former husband, Brian. In the thirteenth-century Icelandic legend, the *Njals saga*, she is portrayed as a Machiavellian-style schemer, instructing her son Sitric to recruit the Viking leaders Sigurd of Orkney and Brodar of Man with the offer of marriage to her and a kingdom in Ireland if they went to battle against Brian.

Gormlaith's royal biography

- Daughter of Murchad mac Finn, king of Leinster from 966 to 972.
- Sister of Máelmórda, king of Leinster who fought against Brian Ború at the Battle of Clontarf.
- Gormlaith's son with King Amlaíb Cuarán, Hiberno-Norse king of Dublin, was Sitric Silkenbeard, king of Dublin between 989 and 1036 (including during the Battle of Clontarf).
- In 981, Gormlaith married Máel Sechlainn mac Domnaill, the high king who defeated Amlaíb at the Battle of Tara (980).
- Gormlaith married Brian Ború. Their son, Donnchad, would go on to succeed him as king of Munster and claim the kingship of Ireland.
- Gormlaith's son Sitric married Brian's daughter, Sláine.
- Gormlaith had a major role in instigating the Battle of Clontarf.
- Gormlaith outlived all her husbands and died in 1030.

Tara and Cashel

Tara and Cashel were both impressive ceremonial centres in the landscape and important centres of early kingships. Heroic kings like Cormac mac Airt, Niall of the Nine Hostages and Conn of the Hundred Battles were associated with Tara. Cashel, likewise, was associated with the heroic kingship of Conall Corc mac Luigthig. He was the founder of the dynasty of the Éoganachta of Munster.

There are similar stories in medieval Irish literature about Conaire Mór of Tara receiving the cloak of kingship and Conall Corc receiving a similar garment. The difference was that the kingship at Cashel was christianized from an early date. This may have involved the combining of prehistoric ceremonies with Christian beliefs.

The Rock of Cashel, Co. Tipperary, is also known as Cashel of the Kings. It is situated on a rocky plateau three hundred feet above the surrounding plain. According to local folklore, the Rock of Cashel was originally in the mountain known as the Devil's Bit. When St Patrick banished Satan from a cave there, the rock landed at Cashel.

Cashel is famous for being one of the most extensive sites of medieval architecture in Ireland. Cormac's Chapel was commisioned by King Cormac mac Cárthaig. The building began in 1127 and was consecrated in 1134. It was built of sandstone in the Romanesque style and probably replaced an earlier timber church.

Muirchertach Ua Briain (d.1119), king of Munster and great-great-grandson of Brian Ború, donated the Rock of Cashel to the church after the Synod of Cashel in 1101. This was part of his ambitious plan to become the most powerful king in Ireland. In 1111 Cashel became an archbishopric. Most of the current buildings on the Rock of Cashel date to the twelfth and thirteenth centuries; from the twelfth century onwards the more important title associated with Cashel was that of archbishop rather than king.

Cormac's Chapel, Cashel

Cashel was the seat of the kings of Munster for hundreds of years

Kings and Christianity at Tara and Cashel

St Patrick and other missionaries attempted to convert kings to Christianity as they were the leaders in society and, therefore, could change the rules and customs of their people. Patrick is said to have converted the king of Munster, Oengus mac Nad Fraích, in 450. By the late-seventh century Tara had been abandoned and the kings were subject to a Christian god. There was no major church built at Tara, in contrast to those at Teltown and Cashel. There was no reference to a church at Tara until the thirteenth century but the site was still important and was used by Uí Néill kings to gain political advantage.

Prophesy: angels and supernatural beings

The status of Tara and Cashel in the medieval period is reflected in contemporary stories. For example, the prophesy of Cuirirán the Swineherd at Cashel arose from his encounter with an angel in a vision, from whom he received knowledge about the future kings of Cashel. This can be compared with Conn of the Hundred Battles of Tara, where a supernatural woman foretold of his birth and the benefits of his reign.

An angel also foretold that the kingship of Munster would be entrusted to whoever first kindled a fire at Cashel. Corc kindled a fire at Dún Cuirc and took possession of Cashel. Another of St Patrick's biographers, Tírechán, included a brief description of Patrick baptizing the grandsons of Conall Corc at Cashel. Muirchú and Tírechán both considered Tara to have been cursed by Patrick.

Tara and Teltown

Teltown superseded Tara in importance with
the coming of Christianity. There was an
important Patrician church situated there
and a synod was held at Teltown where
Columba was excommunicated. In 785
the relics of Erc of Slane were brought there.
The ceremonies at the Rock of Cashel
were also approved of by clerics. This was
not the case at Tara. Unlike Tara, kings
lived in Cashel throughout the medieval
period. They did not live there all year round,
however, as they were obliged to attend
rituals and feasts in different locations.

A pagan burial at Cashel?

One of the medieval kings of Cashel, Óengus
mac Nad Fraích, is said to have been buried
in a standing position, facing his enemies.
This burial was similar to that of Lóegaire
mac Néill at Tara.

Architecture and power

The reuse of prehistoric sites such as
Tara as ceremonial capitals reflected their
continued importance to communities
through the generations. Their physical
solidity and visibility in the landscape
was essential and the long traditions
of kingship were reflected in the
architecture of prehistoric monuments.
The changing nature of kingship in the
medieval period was likewise reflected
in the architecture of Cashel.

The goddess Tailtiu is associated with Teltown

The king's house

Medieval chroniclers were fascinated by prehistory. They sometimes wrote fanciful accounts about the nature and function of monuments such as the Banqueting Hall at Tara. For example, the gaps in each of the parallel banks have been interpreted as entrances to a great hall or as windows. There is a description in the earliest survey of Tara, *Dindgnai Temrach* (*The remarkable places of Tara*), written about 1000:

'It is in the form of a long house, with twelve doors upon it, or fourteen, seven to the west and seven to the east. It is said, that it was here the Feis Temro was held, which seems true; because as many men would fit in it as would form the choice part of the men of Ireland. And this was the great house of a thousand soldiers'.

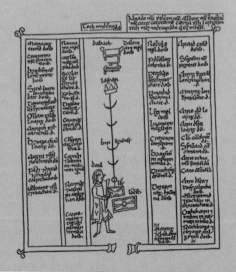

Plan of the Banqueting Hall from the *Book of Leinster*

A royal feast

The Irish name for the Banqueting Hall, *Tech Midhchúarta*, has been translated as the 'House of the mead circuit'. According to the law tracts, royal households visited houses of clients for feasts. The houses had to be large enough to accommodate the king's retinue. Feasting was also associated with ritual occasions.

Function of the Banqueting Hall

It is unlikely that the monument was a Banqueting Hall. Like other monuments on the hill it may have been reused for ceremonial purposes during the medieval period. Some archaeologists speculate that it is not prehistoric and may even have been constructed in the early medieval period.

A rescue excavation that took place at the linear monument at the Knockans (Teltown, Co. Meath) in 1997 and 1998 revealed that the main phase of construction, in the early medieval period, was on top of an Early Iron Age embankment. This shows that this type of prehistoric monument sometimes continued to play an important role in the life of the community in historic times.

The gaps in the Banqueting Hall were thought to be windows or doors of the king's house

What did the king's house look like?

In medieval literature fabulous descriptions of what a king's house might have looked like are found. In the Ulster cycle tale, 'The wooing of Emer', for example, King Conchobar mac Nessa's house at the royal site of Navan Fort, Co. Armagh, is described as follows:

'It was constructed on the plan of the Tech Midhchúarta; there were nine apartments between the hearth and the wall, and each façade was thirty feet high and made of bronze, and there was gold ornamentation everywhere. A royal apartment for Conchobar was erected at the front of the royal house, high above the other couches, and it was ornamented with carbuncles and other precious things: it shone with the radiance of gold and silver and carbuncle and every colour, so that it was as bright by night as by day'.

However, no corresponding archaeological evidence for such a rich royal house at Tara has been discovered.

'YEAH, GREAT BANKS. WHERE'S THE BANQUET?'

Status and the Banqueting Hall

The Banqueting Hall was illustrated in the twelfth-century *Book of Leinster* and also in the fourteenth-century *Yellow Book of Lecan*. In medieval literature it is connected with legal status, political rank and cosmology. Those attending the feast were seated according to their ranks and professions.

Where did the king and his retinue sit?

The Irish law tract on status in society, *Crith Gabhlach*, written c.700, describes the arrangement of a king's house in the early medieval period. The king's bodyguards were ranked according to their social status and also their position in relation to the king. They were located in the southern end of the house, protecting the king. In the northern part of the house the king resided with his wife, his warriors, his spear-holder and his judge. Hostages were chained in the north-eastern part of the house. The rest of the king's retinue, including poets, harpers, pipers, horn players and jugglers were to be found in the southern end of the house, placed according to their status. In the medieval description of the Banquesting Hall, Cormac mac Airt is depicted as the Irish Solomon presiding over his court.

According to the eighth-century law tract on status, *Crith Gablach*, the king's week was organized as follows:

The king's timetable

Sunday: the king drank ale

Monday: the king judged legal cases

Tuesday: the king played board games such as fidchell

Wednesday: the king went hunting

Thursday: the king had sexual relations

Friday: the king went horse-riding

Saturday: the king judged legal cases again

Who did the medieval kings govern?

A king ruled over the *tuath* in medieval Ireland. A *tuath* was a small political unit, defined by a particular territory. It was often bounded by natural features such as bogs, rivers or mountains or by ancestral graves. It is estimated that there were about one hundred *tuatha* in Ireland between the fifth and twelfth centuries. Each province in Ireland including Laigen, Mumu, Connacht, Mide and Ulaid were made up of many *tuatha*. Each province had its own king who was also an over-king. Locally, the *tuath* was the centre of political, religious and social life for the community. Each province had at its centre an ancient capital; these included Tara, Rath-croghan, Uisneach, Knockaulin, Navan Fort and Cashel. The king of Tara was superior to all other provincial kings.

The *tuath*

There were many different classes of people living in the *tuath*. These include the *nemed*, freemen, the unfree, women and slaves. A man's property, learning or skill determined his social class or grade.

Honour price

Under ancient Irish law honour price was a price paid by an offender or the offender's relatives in compensation to an injured person or to the injured person's relatives. It was based on his or her standing in medieval society.

If a person did not behave appropriately he stood to lose part or all of his honour price as his status was dependent on his good name. This would happen if, for example, he committed a crime such as intentionally wounding another person or carrying out an arson attack. If he was involved in very serious criminal activity such as killing one of his own kinsmen then the entire honour price would be lost. Slaves had no status and, therefore, no honour price.

The *nemed*

The *nemed* were a noble class that included kings, poets, bishops, men of ecclesiastical learning and some craftsmen. Each grade of *nemed* had its own honour price. Their grade also affected their legal rights and the size of the retinue which they could have. People of common grades served a variety of lords who were of noble grade. Those professions who had an honour price equivalent to that of the lowest rank of lord included blacksmiths, metal-wrights, physicians and wood-wrights.

The status of people: free and semi-free

There were two classes of freeman, the noble and the common. Both owned their own land. The common freemen served as the base clients of the noble freemen meaning that the common freemen owed the noble freemen payments of labour and food. Carpenters and decorative craftsmen had the same status as common freemen. It was possible to advance within a particular class if more property or skills were acquired. It was much more difficult, if not impossible, to move from one class to another.

Young freemen between the ages of fourteen and twenty belonged to the lowest grade of common freeman. They had not yet established their own houses and were still dependent on their fathers or foster fathers. When they had inherited enough land to support a small herd of about seven cows they moved up a grade. Fishermen, leather workers and comb makers had the same rank as the lowest grade of common freeman.

The semi-free men depended on a landed freeman as they did not own property. Their honour price and status was compromised. Some people who had this status included musicians (except for harpers), jesters and chariot drivers.

Who was the *bóaire*?

The *bóaire* was a prosperous farmer and had landholdings of at least twice that of the young freeman, but was ranked below the noble grades. He was subject to a king and had to supply him with food and labour. However, he also had the legal power to purchase land and so could potentially improve his status. The average *bóaire* owned about twenty cows, six oxen and two bulls. He ploughed the lands with his own plough team and cultivated cereal. He had a corn-drying kiln on his land and access or ownership of a mill. Outhouses on his farm included a pigsty, a calf pen and a barn. He owned two horses, one used for farmwork and the other for riding.

A prosperous farmer's house

The highest ranking *bóaire* was expected to have the resources to welcome a king, a bishop, the head of a monastic school or a judge with their accompanying retinues into his house. He needed a large house to do this – the average size of the *bóaire's* house was about twenty-seven feet in diameter and had a thatched roof. Inside, the floor was covered with rushes. A cauldron with a spit for cooking was on the fire and there was a vat for brewing beer.

Making bread

The *bóaire* and his family ate bread that was made in a kneeding-trough. Iron vessels were used for food and drink. They probably wore sackcloth, a coarse fabric made from goat's hair. At night-time they had candlelight.

The tools

The typical *bóaire* owned lots of tools for use on the farm such as a billhook, a hatchet, an axe, a saw, a knife and spears. The billhook had a sickle-shaped blade with a sharp inner edge, used for pruning branches or clearing the land of thistles and other vegetation. Hatchets and saws were used for cutting down trees and chopping wood. Axes were used for killing livestock, a knife for cutting rushes and spears for hunting. These tools were sharpened on a whetstone.

Other tools for woodworking, such as the adze and the auger, were also used by the *bóaire*. The adze was a type of tool for smoothing or carving wood. It was like an axe but with its cutting edge perpendicular to the handle. The auger was used to drill holes in wood by hand.

'WELL? YOU DON'T WANT ME TO STINK, DO YOU?'

Bathtime

It seems that the average *bóaire* was concerned with personal cleanliness as there is archaeological evidence for washing buckets and bath-tubs in their houses. It is not known, however, how often the *bóaire* had a bath.

Prosperous farmers in the vicinity of the Hill of Tara

There is archaeological evidence for prosperous farmers living and dying in the vicinity of the Hill of Tara in the medieval period. Examples of excavated sites include settlements and cemeteries.

Castlefarm settlement

A medieval settlement site at Castlefarm, near Dunboyne, Co. Meath, was discovered and excavated in 2005 prior to the construction of the M3 roadway. The site was identified as a medieval bivallate enclosure. It consisted of an inner enclosure ditch, an outer enclosure ditch and a southern enclosure annex. Features included numerous pits, spreads and ditches.

Early medieval finds recovered from the site included bone fibula pins, worked antler, glass beads, lignite bracelets, spindle whorls, pottery sherds, tanged iron blades and ringed pins. This demonstrates that it was a high-status site.

Eleven burials were discovered. Seven of the skeletons were lying face upwards, orientated east–west, with no grave goods, suggesting a Christian tradition.

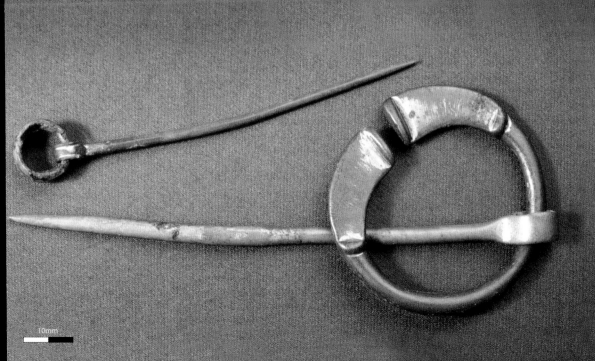

10mm

Roestown

The enclosed medieval site at Roestown, Co. Meath, probably belonged to a farming family of noble rank. It was very rich in artefacts including knife blades, bone combs, pins and needles, glass beads, lignite bracelets, ring pins and stone gaming boards. A souterrain was discovered in the main D-shaped enclosure. It consisted of three beehive chambers linked by three passages with access through a drop-hole entrance.

10mm

Glass beads

5mm

Stone gaming board

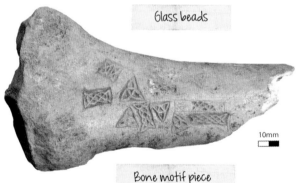

10mm

Bone motif piece

Baronstown

Evidence for domestic activity was found at a ringfort in Baronstown, Co. Meath, when seven kilns for cereal drying were discovered. Ornaments recovered included decorated brooches and a loop-headed pin. Wooden staves from barrels and a bowl with the remains of a substance, probably butter, as well as iron knives, were also found.

Collierstown I

Early medieval cemetery sites near Tara

Early medieval cemetery sites were discovered at Collierstown and Ardsallagh.

Collierstown 1

Collierstown 1, Co. Meath, was originally used before or during the fourth century. A later cemetery for adults was dated to the sixth century. Inhumations in slab-lined graves dating from the fifth to the seventh century may represent Christians buried among pagans. Evidence for pagan practices was discovered alongside post-holes for wooden crosses and a possible earthen shrine. Eight wood-lined graves were also found. The remains of funerary feasts were suggested by the amount of animal bones found at the site.

Ardsallagh

A ring-ditch 13m in diameter was discovered at Ardsallagh. Twenty-three burials were found within it, one in the entranceway and four outside the monument. Archaeologists suggest that these burials date to the seventh century. Ring-ditches are a very common form of prehistoric burial and ritual monument in Ireland and many date to the Bronze Age. A Late Bronze Age vessel containing cremated bone was found a short distance from the ring-ditch.

the king of tara and the poet

the kings of tara had poets in their retinues. a poet was seated in the king's house, according to his status.

importance of the poet

the highest grade of poet in medieval ireland was known as an *ollam*. he was considered a very important person as he was very knowledgeable in the history of the community and his words could confirm the ownership of land. he could recite a satire that would dishonour a king or he could write in praise of a king. as honour was valued in medieval society, satire was greatly feared.

the poet's honour price

the *ollam* was a master-poet and had an honour price equal to that of the king. there were seven grades of independent poet and each grade marked a further skill and mastery over increasingly difficult poetical metres. apprentice poets were still dependent on their masters and the profession of poet was usually hereditary.

did the harper play for the poet?

the harper accompanied recitations of poetry. he had the same honour price as the *bóaire* and was the only musician who had free status.

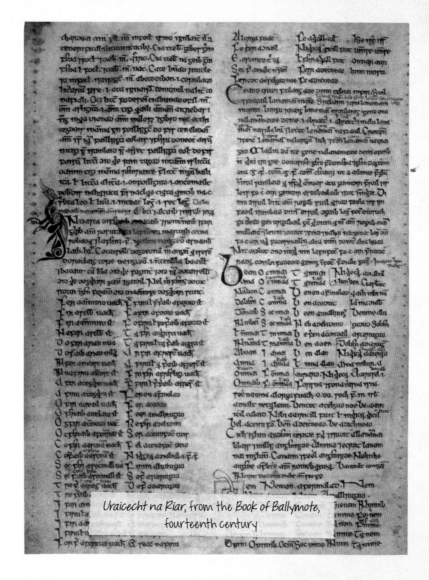

Uraicecht na Ríar, from the Book of Ballymote, fourteenth century

when is a family a family of poets?

In *Uraicecht na Ríar*, an old Irish law text dating to the second half of the eighth century, it was written that 'the answer to this question is not difficult: their father is a poet and their grandfather was a poet.'

The various grades of the poetic order were set out in this text with information on the qualifications and entitlements of each grade, the patronage and appointment of poets and the hereditary nature of the profession.

C.H.S del.ᵗ

Aquatinted by R.Havell.

An Arch Druid in *His Judicial Habit.*

Published June 1, 1815, by R.Havell, 3 Chapel Street, London.

Druids at Tara

Prior to Christianity, a religious caste often known as druids had a lot of influence in religious and political spheres. As they had the ability to predict the future, kings were dependent on the druids to make correct judgements. With the introduction of Christianity some druids moved into the church; those that continued to practice were condemned.

'And all saw the druid being lifted up through the darkness of night almost to the sky, and when he came down again, his body, frozen with hailstones, and snow mixed with sparks of fire, fell to the ground in the sight of all; and the druid's stone is in the south-eastern parts of Tara to the present day, and I have seen it with my own eyes'.

Bishop Tírechán, seventh century

Men of Christian learning

Bishops and men trained in Christian learning (who were not always clerics) were considered very important and had honour prices equivalent to that of the king. Important churches in the Tara region included Trim, Duleek, Dunshaughlin and Ardbraccan.

Queen Lann of Tara

Lann was a queen living in ninth-century Ireland. She was a daughter of Dúngal, the king of Osraige and sister of Cerball, also a king of Osraige (County Kilkenny). Women in the medieval period were dependent on their fathers, brothers or husbands. The honour price of a woman was half that of the person on whom she was dependent. She could inherit land if she had no male siblings; if this happened she had the honour price appropriate to her property. A chief wife had equal status to her spouse. A free woman was entitled to a bed, a saddle and a pet dog.

Wife and mother of kings

Marriages were economic contracts and were also organized for political advantage. Lann's father was given a bride price consisting of land, cattle and household goods for his daughter on her marriage. Even though a woman could not rule in her own right she could be used in power play between kings. She could also retain power for her family through multiple royal marriages.

Multiple marriages

Lann married three times, each time to a king. Her first marriage was to Gáethíne, king of the Loígsi; her second to the king of Tara, Máel Sechlainn mac Maíle Ruanaid, who died in 862; her third was to his successor as king of Tara, Áed Findliath, who died in 879. Lann outlived her three husbands and died in 890.

Complicated family life

She had a complicated family life. Her third husband, Áed Findliath, had left her to marry the daughter of the king of Alba, Máel Muire. Flann Sinna, a king of Tara and Lann's son by Máel Sechlainn mac Maíle Ruanaid, married the widowed Máel Muire. Flann Sinna, therefore, married the widow of his mother's ex-husband, Áed Findliath. To complicate matters further Flann Sinna subsequently married Eithne, a daughter of Áed Findliath.

4: Politics, protests and plans

Tara: the capital of ancient Ireland

Tara is a key archaeological site in terms of national identity in Ireland. This is based on its association with kingship in the medieval period and also on the belief that the site was the burial place of Irish kings in prehistory. Tara was the place of gatherings before battles in the seventeenth century, the scene of a battle in the eighteenth and the location of a political monster meeting in the nineteenth. It was considered by cultural nationalists to be the greatest monument of Ireland's past and capital of an ancient Ireland. William Wilde, the antiquarian and polymath and father of the playwright, Oscar, described how 'the memories of Tara have remained a silver thread in the garment of sackcloth the Irishman has worn for centuries'.

At the end of the nineteenth and the beginning of the twentieth century, Tara became the first site in Ireland to be the focus of a campaign to protect an archaeological monument. Famous writers, artists and politicians, including the Nobelprize-winning poet, W.B. Yeats, attempted to protect 'the most consecrated spot in Ireland'. One hundred years later Seamus Heaney, also a Nobel prize-winning poet, was involved in a protest against the M3 roadway. He wrote that 'it literally desecrates an area – the word means to de-sacralise and for centuries the Tara landscape and the Tara sites have been regarded as part of the sacred ground'. The proclamation of the Irish Republic was read on the Hill of Tara to celebrate the centenary of the Easter Rising on 22 April 2016.

Battles, hostings and assemblies

Hugh O'Neill, Earl of Tyrone, combined forces with Red Hugh O'Donnell and other Gaelic chieftains against Elizabeth I in the Nine Years War (1594–1603). O'Neill supposedly rallied his troops at Tara on their way to Kinsale where they were defeated in a battle in 1601.

An Elizabethan coin was found at Tara near the Mound of the Hostages. One face (top) included an inscription with the words REGINA and ELIZA-BETH with a cross between the two words. On the other face a coat of arms is at the centre with a cross and the date 1581.

Gaelic chiefs and horses at Tara

Gaelic chiefs ceremonially shod their horses at Tara in the sixteenth century. Sir John Perrot, in his *Chronicle of Ireland* (1584–1608), described Hugh O'Neill travelling to Tara where he shod his horse. It was believed that if he could shoe his horse at Tara 'he should be kinge of all Ireland'.

1641

Tara continued to have a potent symbolism because of its association in tradition with high kingship. It was the location of rebel meetings during the 1641 Rebellion that broke out in Ulster in October of that year after Irish Catholic gentry challenged the English administration about their rights as Catholic landowners. This inspired a popular uprising which became an ethnic conflict between the native Catholics on the one hand and the English and Scottish settlers on the other. Tara was an obvious meeting place because of its historical connotations, its church, its geographical position in the middle of Meath and its location on the road from Ulster to Dublin.

Battle of Tara, 1798

The 1798 rebellion, one of the bloodiest conflicts in Irish history, broke out in May of that year. The desire to make Ireland an independent republic was inspired by the French Revolution. It was organized by the United Irishmen, a secretive organization founded in Belfast by Wolfe Tone and others. It was not successful as government forces infiltrated the organization and there was a lack of coordination. Three hundred and fifty rebels were reputedly killed at the Battle of Tara on 26 May 1798.

Illustration of Vinegar Hill, 1798, where British troops crushed the Irish rebellion

A woman of 1798: Molly Weston at Tara

Molly Weston, a Meathwoman, was a leader who was involved in the recruitment and organisation of United Irishmen in the Fingal area in 1798. She rode into the Battle of Tara on a white horse accompanied by her four brothers. Dressed in a green riding costume with gold braid she wore a green cocked hat with a white plume. She was armed with a sword and pistols.

She distinguished herself for her bravery in the battle and led pikemen in repeated charges against the Reagh Fencibles, a volunteer regiment raised for local defence but commanded by regular army officers. A loaded field gun was captured by the insurgents and Molly swung the gun around and killed eleven of the Reagh Fencibles. She and her four brothers were all killed. After the conflict a horse and a lady's side-saddle were found on the battlefield.

Molly Weston was described as handsome and vivacious, quick in mind, active in body and a daring and accomplished horse-woman

Memorials to 1798 Rebels on Tara

The Lia Fáil was moved in 1824 from near the Mound of the Hostages and placed on the central mound of the Forrad to mark the grave of the Irish rebels who died in the Battle of Tara in 1798. Another memorial stone was erected in 1938 alongside the Lia Fáil, also to commemorate those who died in the battle.

Commemorating 1798

On 3 October 1948 a commemoration of the Battle of Tara in 1798 took place. The President of Ireland at the time, Seán T. O'Kelly, was in attendance and Éamon de Valera gave an address.

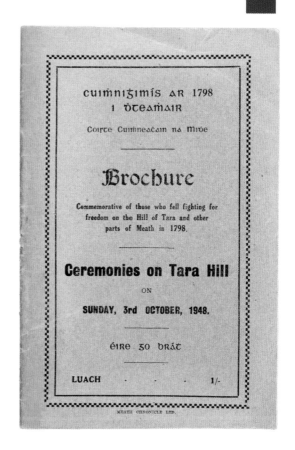

cuimnizimís ar 1798
i dteamair

Coirte Cuimneacáin na Mide

___

Brochure

Commemorative of those who fell fighting for freedom on the Hill of Tara and other parts of Meath in 1798.

___

Ceremonies on Tara Hill

ON

SUNDAY, 3rd OCTOBER, 1948.

éire zo brát

LUACH · · · 1/-

MEATH CHRONICLE LTD.

Daniel O'Connell at Tara

In 1843, Daniel O'Connell, the man credited with the introduction of Catholic Emancipation in 1829, organized a monster meeting on the Hill of Tara. This protest was aimed at pressurizing the British Government to repeal the Act of Union, enacted in 1801. Tara was chosen for this huge protest and political meeting because of its iconic status in Irish history. According to the *Nation* newspaper one milllion people attended the event.

The *Illustrated London News*, 15 August 1843. Banners with images of round towers, wolfhounds and harps were displayed at the 'monster meeting' at Tara. A harper in Bardic dress is in the centre of the picture.

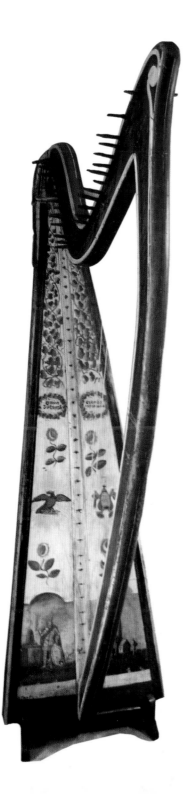

The Drogheda harp

Five students from the Drogheda Harp Society, founded in 1842, played harps to welcome Daniel O'Connell. The Drogheda harp was played by one of the students, William Griffith. This instrument has edges painted in gold and is decorated with images of Brian Ború and the monastic site of Monasterboice. Other motifs include shamrocks encircling the messages 'Eren go-bragh' and 'Eire óg'. 'Eire óg' refers to the group of Young Irelanders led by Thomas Davis who were involved in the *Nation* newspaper.

Tara and the Cultural Revival

The Tara Brooch

The Tara Brooch was made in Ireland in the eighth century, of cast and gilt silver. It is decorated on both faces with gold filigree panels and studs of glass, enamel and amber on the front and with scrolls and triple spirals on the back. A silver chain is attached to the brooch.

Where did the Tara Brooch get its name?

This exquisite ring brooch was found in Bettystown, Co. Meath, in 1850. It came into the ownership of Waterhouse and Company who were jewellers located in Dame Street in Dublin. Waterhouse first published an account of the finding of the Tara Brooch in the pamphlet *Ornamental Irish antiquities: Irish antique brooches* in 1852.

In 1849 the Royal Irish Academy gave permission to Waterhouse to make drawings and copies of their ancient brooches. These Celtic brooches became very fashionable at the time and Waterhouse attached names to the brooches that would increase their market value. Tara, associated with high kings, medieval history, mythology, romance and nationalism, was the best-known example.

Waterhouse agreed to sell the Tara Brooch in 1868. The Royal Irish Academy, which was in the process of buying the Petrie Collection with government aid, received an additional £200 for the purchase of the brooch. Waterhouse made it a condition of the sale that the brooch should never be allowed to leave Ireland. It is now on display in the National Museum of Ireland.

'On the 24th August 1850, a poor woman, who stated that her children had picked it up on the sea shore, offered it for sale to the proprietor of an old iron shop, in Drogheda, who refused to purchase so light and insignificant an article; it was subsequently bought by a watchmaker in the town, who, after cleaning and examining it, proceeded to Dublin, and disposed of it for nearly as many pounds sterling, as he had given pence for it'.

(Waterhouse and Co., *Ornamental Irish antiquities: Irish antique brooches*)

Queen Victoria's Tara Brooch

In 1850 Waterhouse presented the Tara Brooch to Queen Victoria and Prince Albert. It was displayed the following year at the Great Exhibition in the Crystal Palace in London. Copies of it were available for sale and Queen Victoria bought two brooches. Replicas of the Tara brooch were also put on display at the Dublin Great Industrial Exhibition of 1853. At the time it was the largest international event ever to have been held in Ireland. Waterhouse noted that Ireland could boast of 'the continued use of peculiarly national ornaments worn by her princes and nobles in ages long since past'.

'WHAT?... YES OF COURSE IT'S THE REAL ONE.'

The Tara Bracelet

In 1851, Waterhouse made a companion piece, the Tara Bracelet. It was made of silver gilt and had similar motifs to the brooch.

Tara Bracelet, Waterhouse and Co., c.1851

Nationalist groups used the Tara Brooch for their own purposes. For example, Inghinidhe na hÉireann (Daughters of Ireland), founded in 1900 by Maud Gonne, used it as their emblem. Members wore a Tara Brooch on their clothing

St Patrick's Church

St Patrick's Church at Tara was built in the nineteenth century and consists of a simple church and a bell tower. A plaque over the original entrance states that the church was 'rebuilt in 1822'. Some of the architectural features in this church were salvaged from an earlier building, such as the pointed arch window and a memorial plaque to Sir Robert Dillon, soldier and chief justice, dated to 1595. This included the coat of arms of the Dillon family and a Latin inscription. There is also a small carved stone cross with a Tudor rose at its centre mounted in the church.

Evie Hone: stained glass artist

The *Pentecost* window in St Patrick's church at Tara was created by the stained glass artist Evie Hone in 1936. Hone is regarded as one of the twentieth century's greatest artists in this medium. Born in Dublin in 1894, she studied at art colleges in London and also lived in Paris from 1920 to 1932.

Hone was a deeply spiritual artist and her work was inspired by the medieval stained glass in Chartres Cathedral in France and also by the contemporary paintings of George Rouault, a French painter and printer whose work is associated with Fauvism and Expressionism. Fauvism emphasized painterly qualities and strong colours over the representational or realistic.

Hone was to become a pioneer in abstract art in Ireland. She worked for a time in An Túr Gloine, a pioneering cooperative venture, set up in 1903. Six hundred works in stained glass were produced in An Túr Gloine between the years 1903 and 1944. It was a successful enterprise involving mainly Irish women modernist artists.

Evie Hone, Pentecost window, 1936

The harp that once through Tara's halls

The harp that once through Tara's halls
The soul of music shed,
Now hangs as mute on Tara's walls
As if that soul were fled.
So sleeps the pride of former days,
So glory's thrill is o'er;
And hearts that once beat high for praise
Now feel that pulse no more.

No more to chiefs and ladies bright
The harp of Tara swells:
The chord alone that breaks at night
Its tale of ruin tells.
Thus freedom now so seldom wakes,
The only throb she gives
Is when some heart indignant breaks
To show that still she lives!

(Thomas Moore, *Irish Melodies*, Boston, 1854)

The Ark of the Covenant

The British Israelite excavations

The British Israelites dug for the Ark of the Covenant in the Rath of the Synods between the years 1899 and 1902. They began their search at a mound called the 'King's chair' and opened two parallel trenches. This resulted in much damage to the monument.

The Ark of the Covenant was the chest believed to have contained the ten commandments written on stone tablets

The trench exposed under the Rath of the Synods

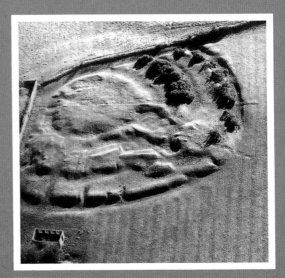

The Rath of the Synods was badly damaged by the British Israelites at the turn of the century

Who were the British Israelites?

The British Israelites believed that white Anglo-Saxons, Americans and possibly Celtic peoples were descended from the Lost Tribes of Israel.

Why did they dig Tara?

The beliefs of the British Israelites were based on the theories of the eighteenth-century antiquarian Charles Vallancey, who argued that Old Irish was derived from Ancient Hebrew. Their views were also based on studies of the Bible, early Irish history, folklore, mythology and Irish literature. These researches led them to conclude that Tara was the 'resuscitated Jerusalem' of a new Israel and they identified the new Israel as the British Empire. They published their conclusions in journals such as the *Covenant People*, the journal of the British Israel Association in London. This organisation was founded by Edward Wheeler Bird, an Anglo-Indian judge, in 1889.

The British Israelites gave their quest to recover the Ark of the Covenant the veneer of science by using the work of archaeologists such as George Petrie. They studied his map of Tara very carefully in an effort to pinpoint the location of the Ark. They produced a copy of it in the *Covenant People*.

Many of those involved in the attempt to recover the Ark of the Covenant were Freemasons.

The Ark of the Covenant features on the Crest of the Grand Lodge, Freemasons' Hall, Dublin

British Israelites based their theories on the work of General Charles Vallancey, an eighteenth-century antiquarian whose work was discredited in his own lifetime

The Egyptian pharoah's daughter

British Israelites believed that the Ark of the Covenant was buried in the grave of Princess Tea Tephi. This Egyptian princess and daughter of a Pharoah makes her first appearance in an eleventh-century Irish poem written by Cuán Ua Lothchan and translated by George Petrie.

According to Irish legend Tea Tephi came to Ireland and married Éirimon, King of Tara. She became so homesick that he built a fort for her on the hill. The British Israelites identified her as a princess from the royal line of the biblical King David who had arrived in Ireland with other Israelites in the sixth century BC. They believed that she was the ancestor of the British Kings and Queens. The British Israelites wanted to recover the Ark and present it to Queen Victoria and later to her son Edward VII.

Media campaign

A media campaign, the first of its kind to protect an archaeological monument, was launched against the British Israelite dig after a visit to the site by Maud Gonne and Arthur Griffith on Christmas Day 1900. Arthur Griffith wrote a series of eleven articles entitled 'Tara of the kings: a sketch of the history of the capital of independent Ireland,' which he published in the *United Irishman* newspaper between 26 July and 4 October 1902.

THE UNITED IRISHMAN

A NATIONAL WEEKLY REVIEW.

No. 1.	MARCH 4th, 1899.	ONE HALFPENNY.
ALL IRELAND.	The Man of the Week.	Calendar for Next Week.

The right to 'stand on the site of the city of their kings'

Arthur Griffith, Douglas Hyde, W.B. Yeats and George Moore visited the Hill of Tara to protest against the British Israelite explorations on 24 June 1902. The landlord, Gustavus Villiers Briscoe, was there drinking a glass of whiskey and directing operations. He was in the company of two men, one of whom had a rifle. W.B. Yeats denounced the 'desecration' of Tara. Griffith insisted that all Irish people had the right to 'stand on the site of the city of their kings'. The man with the rifle put down his gun and stood aside. Griffith, Yeats, Moore and Hyde walked across the Hill of Tara to register their protest.

Douglas Hyde

Arthur Griffith

George Moore

W.B. Yeats

Letter of protest by Hyde, Moore and Yeats

W.B. Yeats, George Moore and Douglas Hyde co-wrote a letter that was published in the *Times* of London on 27 June 1902. They protested that the diggers were working without archaeological supervision and mixing the different layers of earth. It was their view that Tara 'was probably the most consecrated spot in Ireland, and its destruction will leave many bitter memories behind it'.

THE HILL OF TARA.

TO THE EDITOR OF THE TIMES.

Sir,—We have just returned from a visit to the Hill of Tara, where we found that the work of destruction, abandoned a year or two ago, has begun again. Labourers are employed to dig through the mounds and ditches that mark the site of the ancient Royal duns and houses. We saw them digging and shovelling without any supervision, hopelessly mixing the different layers of earth and altering the contour of the hill.

This is not being done through any antiquarian zeal, but, apparently, that the sect which believes the English to be descended from the Ten Tribes may find the Ark of the Covenant.

We are assured that the Commissioners of Public Works in Ireland can do nothing in this case, for by the Ancient Monuments Protection Act of 1882 they can only interfere when the " owner " has himself " constituted " them " the guardians of such monument."

All we can do under the circumstances is to draw the attention of the public to this desecration. Tara is, because of its associations, probably the most consecrated spot in Ireland, and its destruction will leave many bitter memories behind it.

We are, Sir, yours truly,
DOUGLAS HYDE, LL.D.
GEORGE MOORE.
Dublin, June 24. W. B. YEATS.

The Bonfire

On 13 July 1902, the flamboyant nationalist Maud Gonne went with Inghinidhe na hEireann and a party of three hundred children to Tara. Briscoe had prepared a bonfire to honour the coronation of Edward VII.

Maud Gonne thought it would be better to light it in honour of an independent Ireland. So she lit it and sang the rebel song *A Nation Once Again*. The fact that the constabulary were dancing with rage, in her opinion, added greatly to the fun.

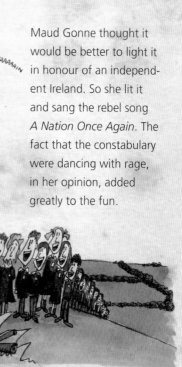

BEST SCHOOL TRIP EVER

Roman coins

The British Israelites did not find the Ark of the Covenant in the Rath of the Synods. They did, however, find fifteen Roman coins of the Emperor Constantine. Constantine the Great ruled the western Roman Empire from 312 to 324. He then became sole emperor until he died in 337. As the coins were not recorded properly by an archaeologist and their position in the stratigraphy noted, information about them was incomplete. There was also debate among archaeologists as to whether the finds were genuine or had been placed there as a hoax. At the time it was common for antiquarians to have their own 'cabinets of curiosities' for the display of their private collections of antiquities. Other Roman objects were recovered from the Rath of the Synods during excavations in the 1950s.

The Ark in modern folklore

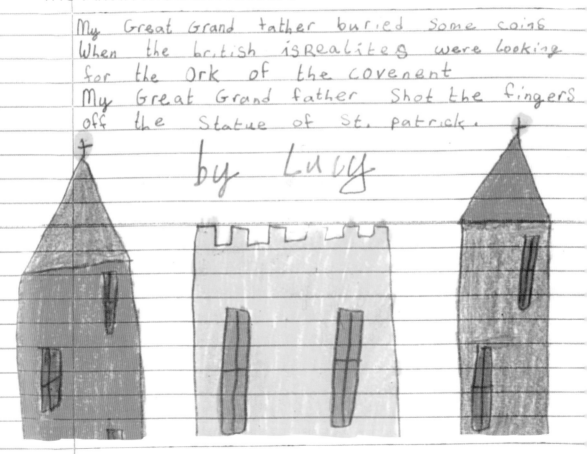

My Great Grand father buried some coins
When the british isRealites were looking
for the Ork of the covenent
My Great Grand father Shot the fingers
off the Statue of St. patrick.

by Lucy

Lucy Wilkinson, Skreen NS, Skreen, Co. Meath (Feb. 2013)

Protests over Patrick

The statue of St Patrick on the Hill of Tara, which was erected in the nineteenth century, was removed because it was damaged in 1992. A competition for a new statue of St Patrick was held in 1996. The winner was Annette Hennessy of Belfast who sculpted an eight-foot bronze statue. However, this new St Patrick did not meet with local approval. The matter was discussed in the Dáil on 13 March 1997. Noel Dempsey TD made the point that 'It is a source of annoyance to the local community that the episcopal representation of St Patrick should be replaced by a statue depicting a young boy dressed as a swineherd on the Hill of Tara'. The Minister of State at the Department of Arts, Culture and the Gaeltacht, Pat Carey, shared the sculptor's explanation of her ideas about St Patrick as follows:

'My sculpture is not a traditional-type statue of St Patrick but speaks of the myth and magic associated with the many folk legends which have come down to us. The sculpture depicts the man who fought druids with fire, who was said to have been untouched by rain, who could light up the dark with his fingers, and who changed himself and his followers into deer, to escape from the high king Lóegaire and his Druids on the Hill of Tara'.

Dempsey replied 'That is paganism'.

Controversial sculpture of St Patrick is defended

Tara and the M3 motorway

The controversy

The controversy that erupted in response to the building of the M3 motorway through the Tara/Skreen valley at the beginning of the twenty-first century mirrored that of the British Israelite controversy one hundred years previously in that it involved leading intellectuals, politicians, writers and artists. The context of the British Israelite episode was the Cultural Revival and its competing identities before Ireland achieved independence. The context of the M3 controversy was the Celtic Tiger era (1995–2005), reflecting tensions between the protection of cultural heritage and economic imperatives.

Defining the Tara landscape

The controversy centred on the definition of the 'Tara landscape'. Those in favour of the construction of the M3 interpreted it as the monuments on the hill that were in state ownership. Those opposed, based on recent research, argued that monuments in the wider landscape surrounding the hill were an essential part of the Tara ritual complex. This meant that a motorway would compromise this historic and cultural landscape.

An Environmental Impact Statement was commissioned as a precursor to the building of the roadway. Its findings included a list of the sites and monuments identified along the M3 path. These were perceived as isolated from the context of the wider Tara landscape, an interpretation which proved to be the kernel of the ensuing controversy.

Dáil sub-committee on the Hill of Tara, 16 Dec. 2004

World status of Tara

Tara's status as an archaeological site of national and world significance was reflected in the length of the Bord Pleanála hearing. It was one of the longest in the history of the state and lasted twenty-eight days. On 25 August 2003 a decision in favour of the proposed motorway was published. A year later, *The National Monuments Amendment Act* was introduced which gave the government the power to authorize the destruction of a national monument if it was deemed to be in the public interest.

Tara: the hot topic

The topic of Tara and the M3 became hotly debated in newspapers in Ireland and around the globe. There were debates in both Houses of the Oireachtas and a presentation was given by experts to the Oireachtas Committee on the Environment. Letters were written to politicians of all parties. Reports were commissioned, documents prepared for discussion and letters objecting to the planning application lodged. Court cases ensued. In 2008, Tara was placed on the World Monuments Watch List of 100 Most Endangered Sites.

Academics worldwide signed declarations against the M3 motorway. Thousands of ordinary people got involved, signing online petitions and participating in numerous protests and marches.

Opinions worldwide

There was professional uneasiness about the decision to go ahead with the controversial M3 motorway. Academics from Ireland, the UK, the US, Canada, Germany, the Netherlands, Scandinavia, Croatia and Russia got involved. Learned bodies worldwide, including the European Association of Archaeologists, the Archaeological Institute of America and the Smithsonian, objected to the plan.

Muireann Ní Bhrolcháin
(lecturer in Early Irish, NUI Maynooth,
and a member of Save the
Tara/Skreen Valley Group)

Those leading the campaign in Ireland included the archaeologists Conor Newman and Joe Fenwick, the early Irish historian Edel Bhreathnach, the lecturer in Early Irish Muireann Ní Bhrolcháin (Save the Tara/Skreen Valley Group), Julitta Clancy of the Meath Archaeological and Historical Society and Vincent Salafia of TaraWatch. Other heritage bodies such as the Royal Irish Academy, The Discovery Programme, the Royal Society of Antiquaries of Ireland and the Heritage Council expressed their opinions about the impact of the proposed road on such an important site.

'The Hill of Tara is only the core area of a much larger archaeological and cultural landscape'.

Professor George Eogan, *Smithsonian Magazine*, 1 March 2009

Writers, artists and musicians against the M3

Famous writers, artists, musicians and actors who lent their voices and talents to the campaign against the construction of a road through the Tara landscape included the Nobel laureate and poet Seamus Heaney, the Pulitzer prize-winning poet Paul Muldoon, the writer Colm Toibin, the artists Jim Fitzpatrick and Robert Ballagh, the musicians Laoise Kelly and Steve Cooney, the actor Stuart Townsend and the Oscar-winning actress Charlize Theron.

Seamus Heaney at Heritage Week event, 2010

Tara: an ideal

'It's a word that conjures an aura – it conjures up what they call in Irish *dúchas*, a sense of belonging, a sense of patrimony, a sense of an ideal, an ideal of the spirit if you like, that belongs in the place and if anywhere in Ireland conjures that up it's Tara...'

'If ever there was a place that deserved to be preserved in the name of the dead generations from pre-historic times up to historic times up to completely recently – it was Tara.'

Seamus Heaney

On the summer solstice of 2005 thousands of ordinary people assembled on Tara

DOWN WITH THIS SORT OF THING

Tara of the kings
by Paul Muldoon

We met at the summer solstice
When everything stood still
Her sloping away like Iseult
Left me over the hill
I raised the chamber in the mound
The oak-fringed sacred spring
That feeds the streams that run around
Tara of the kings.

She was through with carbon dating
Stakeholders with no hair
She was through with monster meetings
In flats off Parnell Square
She was through with crowned and uncrowned
Yew trees with countless rings
The ditch that used to run around
Tara of the kings.

Could we who endured the Penal
And Edward Poyning's Laws
(Never mind the Beef Tribunal)
Now somehow be in awe
Of a road running through the ground
On which stood our althing
And not ensure it run around
Tara of the kings?

The Pulitzer prize-winning poet,
Professor Paul Muldoon, reading
in the churchyard at Tara

We know the stone of destiny
Was set up in this soil
Now the soldiers of destiny
Are set to bank the spoils
And lest they wish to be renowned
For rape and ravishing
They'll not give us the runaround
On Tara of the kings.

We're fated to be remembered
As spoilers of the dead
And though we seem quite unhampered
By honour or by dread.

Yet we are dread- and honour-bound
To our unborn offspring
To ensure the M3 run around
Tara of the kings.

A living human sculpture on the Hill of Tara: over 1,500 people protesting against the M3 (Sept. 2007). The M3 was opened by the Minister for Transport, Noel Dempsey TD on 4 June 2010 despite protests

The restoration of Tara

The musician Annie W. Patterson, co-founder of the *Feis Ceoil* and composer of the opera 'The High-King's daughter' suggested that Tara should be restored in an article published in the *Journal of the Ivernian Society* in July 1908. In her fanciful plan a stone and mortar Hall of Song would be built on the site of the Banqueting Hall. A residential Irish art college, a Tara picture gallery for the exhibition of native art and a printing press would be established nearby. Also included in the plan were offices for use by the National Literary Society and the Gaelic League and classrooms for the teaching of the Irish language.

The new city of Tara

In the 1940s a radical nationalist political party, *Ailtirí na hAiséirghe* (Architects of the Resurrection) proposed a programme for what it termed 'the new order in the new Ireland' which included a proposal to reconstruct Tara as the capital city of Ireland.

This was because they believed that Tara was the centre of the 'free, Gaelic and exemplary Christian state' of the future. The architect Daithí Ó hÁinle, who later designed the Garden of Remembrance in Dublin and the Basilica at Knock, drew up the outline plans for the new city of Tara in 1942.

It would have a 'column of the Resurrection' as its centrepoint, with a new national university, a cathedral, a theatre, a stadium, a 'Garden of Heroes' and a 'Great National Avenue'. Ó hÁinle wrote that this new restoration of Tara would prove that 'we were in earnest in our intention to create for ourselves a fresh new world in Ireland'.

The article about the new city of Tara was published in the journal *Aiséirghe* in 1942.

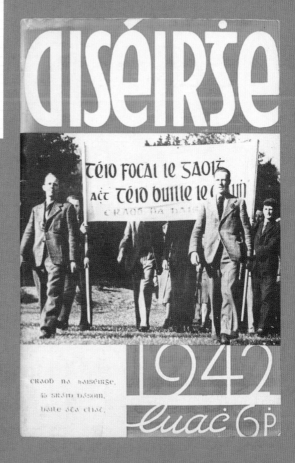

off

off

off

off

off

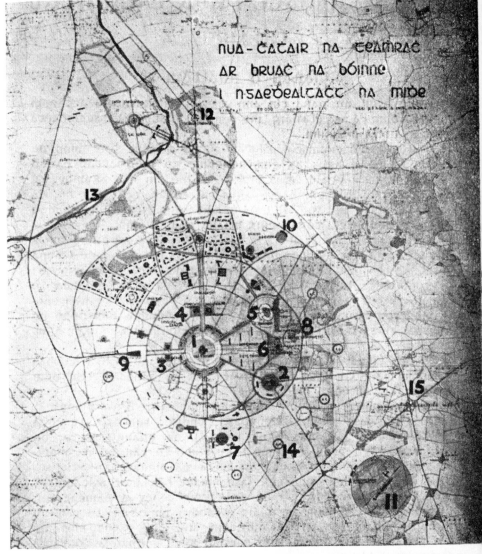

NUA-ĊAṪAIR NA TEAṀRAĊ
AR BRUAĊ NA BÓINNE
I NGAEḊEALTAĊT NA MIḊE

1. Cuar-Ṗáirc (Dáil Éireann).
2. Árd-Eaglais.
3. Halla na Caṫraċ.
4. Amarclann Náisiúnta, Árus Scannán, Pioctúrlann, Ceol-Dráma.
5. Spórt-Stadium—Áit Toilteann.
6. Laoċ-Ġarrḋaiḋ Náisiúnta. Columan na hAiséirġe.
7. Iarsmalann Béaloiḋeosa Faoi'n spéir.
8. Cnoc na Teaṁraċ.
9. Stáisiún Traenaċ.
10. Iolscoil Náisiúnta.
11. Aerlongṗort.
12. An Bóinn.
14. Aonaiḋ Cómarsanaċta.
15. Croscaire Mór.

45

The architect Daithí Ó hAinle's plan for the city of Tara in 1942

NEW CITY OF TARA ON THE BANKS OF THE BOYNE IN THE GAELTACHT OF MEATH

1. The Dáil
2. Cathedral
3. City Hall
4. National Theatre
5. Sports Stadium
6. Column of the Resurrection
7. Open-air Folklife Museum
8. Hill of Tara
9. Train Station
10. National University
11. Airport
12. The River Boyne
14. Neighbourhood Units
15. Big Crossroads

Restoring Tara in the 1970s

In the 1970s a wealthy American of Irish heritage sent a proposal to Taoiseach Jack Lynch for the restoration of Tara. The proposed project 'For Ireland far reaching designs' included moving the Dáil to Tara, building an avenue between the Hill of Tara and the Hill of Slane and the establishing of a university at Tara.

William Edward Patrick O'Donnell offered first $5,000 and later $100,000 for his plan to be put into effect. He believed that 'people of Irish blood the world around will be proud to contribute to a cause which will add to Ireland's glory'. His proposal was turned down and he was encouraged to use his money for 'some other worthy case' in Ireland.

Moving the Dáil to Tara

O'Donnell felt that as the capital of Ireland stood 'on the sacred soil of Tara' for nearly three thousand years when it was a united country, representatives of all-Ireland should be seated in one parliament on the Hill of Tara.

St Patrick's walk

In his pamphlet O'Donnell wrote: 'let every Irish man and woman, appeal to the Dáil, to nationalize the Hills of Tara and Slane'. He wanted this so that an avenue, 'St Patrick's walk', could be built to connect the Hill of Slane with St Patrick's statue on the Hill of Tara.

Tara University

He thought that a University of Tara should be established by Catholic monks. As Irish people had at one time been 'the educators of Europe', the proposed university on the Hill of Tara could become 'an agency of hope for the human race'.

Tara: a beacon light

O'Donnell wrote that 'Ireland is the heart; but the body of the Irish race extends around the world'. This idea of modern Ireland and its diaspora echoes the traditional one of Tara being at the centre of the world. His idealistic and fanciful ideas perhaps reflect a desire to return to the land in general, and Tara in particular, as a solution to the problems of the modern world. It was as if it was safe to embrace modernity by first reconnecting to the past. According to him, Tara would be 'a beacon light to a world floundering in its efforts to maintain its moral equilibrium'

Sacred national ground

Throughout prehistory and history people have continued to return to the Hill of Tara for political and cultural reassurance. Tara was regarded as the capital of Ireland prior to independence and an important place of assembly throughout history. It is considered to be sacred national ground.

POBLACHT NA H EIREANN.
THE PROVISIONAL GOVERNMENT
OF THE
IRISH REPUBLIC
TO THE PEOPLE OF IRELAND.

IRISHMEN AND IRISHWOMEN: In the name of God and of the dead generations from which she receives her old tradition of nationhood, Ireland, through us, summons her children to her flag and strikes for her freedom.

Having organised and trained her manhood through her secret revolutionary organisation, the Irish Republican Brotherhood, and through her open military organisations, the Irish Volunteers and the Irish Citizen Army, having patiently perfected her discipline, having resolutely waited for the right moment to reveal itself, she now seizes that moment, and, supported by her exiled children in America and by gallant allies in Europe, but relying in the first on her own strength, she strikes in full confidence of victory.

We declare the right of the people of Ireland to the ownership of Ireland, and to the unfettered control of Irish destinies, to be sovereign and indefeasible. The long usurpation of that right by a foreign people and government has not extinguished the right, nor can it ever be extinguished except by the destruction of the Irish people. In every generation the Irish people have asserted their right to national freedom and sovereignty; six times during the past three hundred years they have asserted it in arms. Standing on that fundamental right and again asserting it in arms in the face of the world, we hereby proclaim the Irish Republic as a Sovereign Independent State, and we pledge our lives and the lives of our comrades-in-arms to the cause of its freedom, of its welfare; and of its exaltation among the nations.

The Irish Republic is entitled to, and hereby claims, the allegiance of every Irishman and Irishwoman. The Republic guarantees religious and civil liberty, equal rights and equal opportunities to all its citizens, and declares its resolve to pursue the happiness and prosperity of the whole nation and of all its parts, cherishing all the children of the nation equally, and oblivious of the differences carefully fostered by an alien government, which have divided a minority from the majority in the past.

Until our arms have brought the opportune moment for the establishment of a permanent National Government, representative of the whole people of Ireland and elected by the suffrages of all her men and women, the Provisional Government, hereby constituted, will administer the civil and military affairs of the Republic in trust for the people.

We place the cause of the Irish Republic under the protection of the Most High God, Whose blessing we invoke upon our arms, and we pray that no one who serves that cause will dishonour it by cowardice, inhumanity, or rapine. In this supreme hour the Irish nation must, by its valour and discipline and by the readiness of its children to sacrifice themselves for the common good, prove itself worthy of the august destiny to which it is called.

Signed on Behalf of the Provisional Government,
THOMAS J. CLARKE,
SEAN Mac DIARMADA,   THOMAS MacDONAGH,
P. H. PEARSE,   EAMONN CEANNT,
JAMES CONNOLLY.   JOSEPH PLUNKETT

Tara and the Proclamation

Patrick Pearse had expressed a wish that the Proclamation should be read on the Hill of Tara on Easter Sunday, 1916. The man given the task of organising this was Donal O'Hannigan, the leader of the Irish Volunteers in Louth. The plan was that the Dundalk Volunteers would gather arms and march towards Tara. They were to be joined by comrades in Ardee and Dunleer and then to march to Tara where the Proclamation was to be read. They would then march to Blanchardstown in Dublin where they would be joined by Volunteers in Meath and Wicklow. When the order for the Rising was counter-manded by Eoin MacNeill this did not happen.

On the centenary of the Rising, relatives of the Dundalk Volunteers who mobilized for the Easter Rising were in attendance at Tara for the reading of the proclamation on Easter Monday, 28 March 2016. This cultural event was organized by the Meath County Board of *Comhaltas Ceoltóirí Éireann*. It included Irish music and dance, a *teach Gaeilge*, Gaelic games, talks on Irish history and the viewing of artefacts from 1916.

A centenary reading of the Proclamation on the Hill of Tara by Donal O'Hannigan, grandson of the Irish Volunteer who received the order to do so from Patrick Pearse in 1916

5: The study of Tara

Nineteenth-century scholars on Tara

In the nineteenth century antiquarians and archaeologists became interested in Tara, identified as the ancient capital and seat of the high kings of Ireland. A systematic study of the monuments and an exploration of medieval literature was embarked upon. For antiquarians and cultural nationalists the medieval period represented a time when Ireland was independent and free of the shackles of the British Empire.

The antiquarian William R. Wilde published *The beauties of the Boyne, and its tributary, the Blackwater* in 1849. A renowned eye and ear surgeon in Dublin, Wilde was also a polymath whose interests spanned history, archaeology, folklore, art history and travel.

Wilde's description of the Banqueting Hall

Wilde described the Banqueting Hall at Tara in terms that reflected the influence of nineteenth-century romantic nationalism on his writings. His description influenced later scholars in their archaeological interpretations of this monument:

'Here sat in days of yore kings with golden crowns upon their heads; warriors with brazen swords in their hands; bards and minstrels with their harps; grey-bearded ollamhs; druids with their oak-leaf crowns; learned historians; wise brehons and subtle lawyers; the physi-cians; the smiths, artificers, charioteers, huntsmen, architects; the chess-players and cup-bearers, together with crowds of servants and retainers, whose places are all specified in the ancient annals relating to Tara'

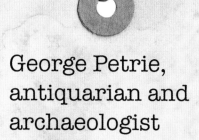

George Petrie, antiquarian and archaeologist (1790–1866)

George Petrie was a famous nineteenth-century antiquarian. Antiquarians studied a variety of subjects including history, literary sources, languages and artefacts in order to understand the past.

George Petrie

Petrie's collection

Like other nineteenth-century antiquarians Petrie collected antiquities. His collection was described in the *Dublin University Magazine* (December 1839) as 'the most curious and interesting of its kind in the world'. By the time he died in 1866, his collection consisted of 1,372 objects and was bought for the Royal Irish Academy Museum. Petrie's antiquities eventually became part of the national collection in the National Museum of Ireland.

Contemporary description of Petrie

'*Here we have one of the most interesting men of the age, surrounded by an elegant number of books, old armour, musical instruments, and drawings, characteristic of his varied accomplishments as a painter, musician, antiquarian, and man of letters*'.

Dublin University Magazine (December 1839).

Cabinets of curiosities were fashionable in the nineteenth century. They reflected the collecting focus of archaeology in the nineteenth century before the development of scientific archaeology

Father of Irish archaeology

Petrie has been described as the father of Irish
archaeology because his methods were at the
beginnings of the discipline of scientific archaeology and his studies were scrupulous for that time.
He combined archaeological and historical
evidence very effectively. He also contributed
articles on archaeological topics regularly to the
Dublin Penny Journal, bringing the subject to a
wider reading public.

St Patrick's Bell is from Petrie's collection. He wrote
that the sound of the bell 'heralded the advent of
Christianity to the Isle of Saints'. However, this bell
was dated to the eighth–ninth century

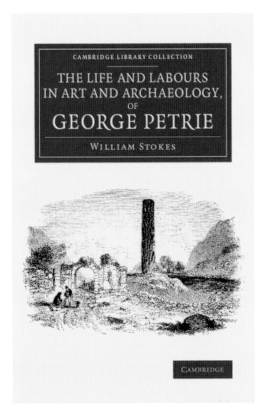

In Petrie's studies 'the monument verifies the history
and the history identifies the monument, and both
become mutually illustrative'. William Stokes,
*The life and labours in art and archaeology
of George Petrie*

Shrine of St Patrick's Bell

First interdisciplinary study of Tara

In 1839 George Petrie expressed the view that even though the ancient splendour of Tara had been the theme of most modern Irish antiquarians and historians, their work had resulted in 'little light either on its past state or existing remains, and have made but little impression on the minds of the learned'. He changed this when he published a significant paper entitled 'On the history and antiquities of Tara Hill' in the *Transactions of the Royal Irish Academy*. This detailed paper was the first interdisciplinary study of Tara, drawing on *Dindshenchas Érenn*, which was compiled in the eleventh and twelfth centuries, and also on the recent work carried out by John O'Donovan of the Ordnance Survey.

Ordnance Survey

George Petrie was superintendent of the topographical department of the Ordnance Survey of Ireland from 1835 to 1842. Other pioneering scholars who worked in this department included John O'Donovan and Eugene O'Curry, both of whom influenced Petrie's archaeological work. John O'Donovan was a Celtic scholar with a knowledge of Irish, Latin and Greek. He included important descriptive details about archaeological monuments and topography in his fieldwork for the Ordnance Survey. He was the first to write about some of the main monuments at the royal site of Rathcroghan and his Ordnance Survey letters are still used by modern archaeologists.

Eugene O'Curry was a self-taught scholar who was involved in the copying, cataloguing and translation of ancient Irish manuscripts. He was appointed to the first chair of Irish History and Archaeology at the Catholic University of Ireland, founded by John Henry Newman in 1854. This was the second professorship in archaeology established in Britain and Ireland, the first being the Disney Chair of Archaeology at Cambridge University in 1851.

Newman had stipulated that the archaeological department should be involved in the study of the language, remains, manuscripts of ancient Ireland 'with special reference to its Catholicity'. O'Curry bore this in mind in his publications, noting in his book *Lectures on the manuscript materials of ancient Irish history* that there was evidence of 'the faith and devotion of her people, preserved with heroic constancy through ages of the most crushing oppression'. O'Curry tried, often unsuccessfully, to correlate artefacts with materials described in the texts.

John O'Donovan (1806–61)

1845: *Grammar of the Irish language*

1847: Translation of *Leabhar na gCeart* (*The Book of Rights*) for the Celtic Society

1848–51: Publication of seven-volume *Annals of the Four Masters*

1849: Appointed to chair of Celtic languages in Queens College Belfast

Eugene O'Curry (1794–1862)

1854: Appointed to the chair of Irish History and Archaeology at the Catholic University of Ireland

1861: *Lectures on the manuscript materials of ancient Irish history*

1873: *On the manners and customs of the ancient Irish*

Petrie: winner of RIA gold medal for his paper on Tara

Petrie was awarded the prestigious Royal Irish Academy gold medal for the publication of his paper on Tara. He sent a copy of it to Thomas Moore, composer of the song, 'The harp that once through Tara's halls'. Between 1899 and 1902, British Israelites studied Petrie's map of Tara very carefully in an effort to pinpoint the location of the Ark of the Covenant. They produced a copy of it in their journal, the *Covenant People*.

Later scholars made more productive use of Petrie's ground-breaking research. It is still an important source for archaeologists and historians studying Tara today.

THE

TRANSACTIONS

OF THE

ROYAL IRISH ACADEMY.

VOL. XVIII.

DUBLIN:
PRINTED BY R. GRAISBERRY,
PRINTED TO THE ROYAL IRISH ACADEMY.
SOLD BY HODGES & SMITH, DUBLIN;
AND BY T. & W. BOONE, LONDON.
M.DCCC.XXXIX.

R.A.S. Macalister (1870–1950)

R.A.S. Macalister, a pioneering Irish archaeologist in the late nineteenth and early twentieth century and the first professor of Celtic Archaeology at University College Dublin (from 1909–43), was the leading expert on Tara during that period. He was also a biblical archaeologist and was employed earlier by the Palestine Exploration Fund to lead excavations in Palestine. This resulted in his publication *The excavation of Gezer* (three volumes) in 1912.

While his methods were criticized by later archaeologists, Macalister was described by Jonathan Tubb of the British Museum and president of the Palestine Exploration Fund as 'an archaeologist who can rightly be described as an intellectual giant'. He served a term as president of the Royal Society of Antiquaries of Ireland (1924–28) and as president of the Royal Irish Academy (1926–31).

Macalister had strongly opposed the British Israelite excavations on Tara between 1899 and 1902 and described the digging as an 'offence against science and against reason' in his paper 'Temair Breg: a study of the remains and traditions of Tara', published in the *Proceedings of the Royal Irish Academy* (1917–19). He regarded this study as an update of George Petrie's monograph and corrected some of Petrie's interpretations of the *Dindshenchas*. In his book he explored topography, origin, kingship, gods and cults, the Lia Fáil and the place of Tara in European culture.

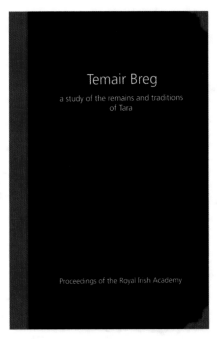

Temair Breg

a study of the remains and traditions of Tara

Proceedings of the Royal Irish Academy

A pagan sanctuary of ancient Ireland

Macalister's book *Tara: a pagan sanctuary of ancient Ireland*, published in 1931, was an extended version of his paper. It was generally well received. Eoin MacNeill, Macalister's contemporary and the first Professor of Early Irish History (including medieval) at University College Dublin, wrote in his review that 'we cannot question the main thesis that Tara, besides being a great political and social centre, was also a great religious centre in pre-Christian Ireland'.

The eminent historian Goddard H. Orpen praised Macalister's book in *The English Historical Review* (1933) as 'as a handy book which can be read anywhere and could be carried on to the hill itself'. He also pointed out that 'we cannot expect to learn much more about Tara without a scientific excavation of the principal sites'.

TARA: A PAGAN SANCTUARY OF ANCIENT IRELAND

The American anthropologist and Assistant Professor of Archaeology at Yale, George Grant MacCurdy, in a review published in the *American Journal of Archaeology*, acknowledged that '*Dindshenchas*, compiled about 1,000 years ago, is indispensable for the topography of Tara'. Macalister included aerial photographs in his book, a first in Irish archaeology, which enhanced the study of the topography of the site.

Teamhair: Tara

In 1935 Macalister wrote the text for *Teamhair: Tara*, one of the official guides to national monuments published by the Office of Public Works in Dublin. It contained a brief description of the main visible monuments.

Tara broadcast

On 8 April 1937 Macalister made a radio broadcast from the top of the Mound of the Hostages in an innovative attempt to bring knowledge about Tara to the general public. A national broadcasting station had been opened in Athlone by De Valera in 1933 and Macalister was keen to make use of the medium for the promotion of archaeology. He was interviewed on Tara by District Justice Liam Price. Price asked Macalister about the possibility of a scientific excavation of Tara. Macalister replied that 'Tara is one of the most important historical sites in Europe. And its proper excavation should be a national undertaking of the highest importance'. Macalister also expressed the view that Tara was not 'merely national' but 'belongs to the whole world'.

R.A.S. Macalister (on left) broadcasting from Tara in 1937

The first scientific excavations of Tara

●●●●●●●●●●●●●●●●

'Should Hill of Tara be excavated?'

When it was announced that there was a government initiative to excavate Tara in the 1950s, controversy erupted in the newspapers. The diplomat and archaeologist Eoin MacWhite published an article in the *Irish Times* on 2 February 1952 under the heading 'Should Hill of Tara be excavated?'. He wrote that 'The British Israelites knew no better, but we profess to have a proper realisation of the value of our ancient and historical monuments, and try to protect them by legislation'.

Reservations

MacWhite expressed the opinion that 'Until we have attained a universally recognised high standard of excavation technique, we would be well advised to apply our efforts on less crucial sites and win our archaeological spurs before tackling Tara'.

Seán P. Ó Ríordáin: a major figure in European archaeology

The archaeologist tasked with the excavation of Tara was Seán P. Ó Ríordáin. He succeeded Macalister as Professor of Celtic Archaeology at University College Dublin, serving from 1943 to 1957, a position for which MacWhite was an unsuccessful applicant. Unlike Macalister and antiquarians of the nineteenth century, Ó Ríordáin was a Catholic from a working class background. He received his archaeological training from Canon Power at University College Cork, at the National Museum under the Austrian archaeologist Adolf Mahr and abroad at universities in Britain, Scandinavia and continental Europe. Ó Ríordáin was described by Glyn Daniel, an eminent Welsh scientist and archaeologist who became the Disney Professor of Archaeology at Cambridge, as 'a major figure in European archaeology'.

Dáil question

A response to a Dáil question posed by James M. Dillon, prompted by the MacWhite article, listed the number of excavation licences that had been issued to Ó Ríordáin. Examples included Ballycatten Fort, Co. Cork; Lough Gur, Co. Limerick; earthworks at the Curragh, Co. Kildare; a megalithic tomb at Ballyedmonduff, Co. Dublin; and a ringfort at Letterkeen, Co. Mayo.

Turning the sod

The Taoiseach, Éamon de Valera, turned the sod on the excavations at Tara on 21 June 1952 amid much press coverage. Many dignitaries attended the event. It was reported in the *Irish Press* that only Irish was spoken at the ceremony.

Telegram from Oxford

The famous archaeologist, Christopher Hawkes, sent a telegram to De Valera from Oxford on 19 June 1952:

PLEASE ACCEPT MY SINCERE CONGRATULATIONS FOR IRELAND ON ENTERPRISE TARA EXCAVATORS AND YOUR INAUGURATING THEM TOMORROW PERSONALLY AS TAOISEACH. THIS FINE LEAD TO HISTORY AND SCIENCE WILL BE APPRECIATED EVERYWHERE AND AS PRESIDENT PREHISTORIC SOCIETY I WISH IRISH SCHOLARSHIP ALL PROSPERITY AND YOUR GIFTED EXCAVATORS ALL SUCCESS.

Professor S.P. Ó Ríordáin with map of Tara

Christopher Hawkes visited the excavations in August 1953. Other famous visitors included the Scottish archaeologist Sir Mortimer Wheeler and the Australian prehistorian Gordon V. Childe, both from the Insitute of Archaeology, University College London.

Éamon de Valera turning the sod at Tara, 21 June 1952

Scientific excavation

Despite the misgivings of some, Ó Ríordáin conducted the first scientific excavations at Tara. He began his work at the Rath of the Synods in 1952 and continued with another season of excavation in 1953. After that, he dug a trench across the ditch of Ráith na Rí. He proceeded to excavate the Mound of the Hostages but died prematurely in 1957 at the age of fifty-two. It was many decades later before his results were published.

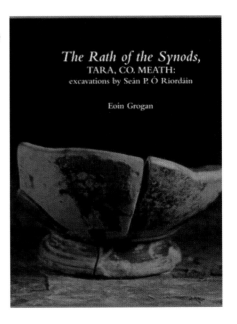

In 1997, Helen Roche, on behalf of The Discovery Programme, reopened the cuttings that Ó Ríordáin had made across Ráith na Rí between the years 1952 and 1955. The results were very important as the enclosure was dated to the first century BC. Evidence for bronze and iron and possible glassworking was also discovered. *The Rath of the Synods, Tara, Co. Meath: excavations by Seán P. Ó Ríordáin* was published by Eoin Grogan in 2008.

The BBC filmed work at the Mound of the Hostages in 1956

Discovery of passage tomb

It was Ó Ríordáin who discovered the existence of the passage tomb under the Mound of the Hostages during excavations in 1955 and 1956. He published his paper 'A burial with faience beads at Tara', in the *Proceedings of the Prehistoric Society* in 1955 and a pamphlet entitled *Tara – the monuments on the hill* in 1957. He participated in the BBC television programme *Buried Treasure* in 1956 and a special broadcast on Tara was aired which focussed on the discovery of the burial of the 'Boy-King'.

The passage tomb in the Mound of the Hostages was not as big as Newgrange but no comparable site in Ireland or in Europe had produced such a rich assemblage of artefacts.

Meticulous record-keeping

In his publication of the excavations in 2005, Professor Muiris O'Sullivan of UCD praised the work of Ó Ríordáin and his successor, Ruaidhrí de Valera, who completed a season of excavation at the Mound of the Hostages:

'It is a tribute to the meticulous record-keeping of Ó Ríordáin and his team, carried on by De Valera and others, that it has been possible to reconstruct so much of what was discovered. Virtually, the entire body of material from the site has remained intact'.

Duma na nGiall
TARA
The MOUND of the HOSTAGES
Muiris O'Sullivan

Ruaidhrí de Valera (1916–78)

Ruaidhrí de Valera, son of Taoiseach Éamon de Valera, was appointed Professor of Celtic Archaeology at UCD in 1957. He worked previously as a lecturer in Old Irish and Welsh at Maynooth University, followed by a stint as place-names officer and subsequently archaeological officer at the Ordnance Survey. He was an expert on megalithic tombs and co-published the *Survey of the megalithic tombs of Ireland* (3 vols; 1961, 1964 and 1971).

Aerial photography

It was the opinion of the British prehistorian and pioneer of aerial photography, O.G.S Crawford, that it provided for archaeology 'a means of research as valuable as the telescope for the astronomer'.

This method of obtaining high-level views of an historic environment facilitates the identification of new sites that could not be discovered at ground level and contributes to the understanding and interpretation of historic landscapes. This technique also demonstrates the value of non-invasive archaeology. Aerial photographs were taken of Tara between 1969–71 by Kenneth St Joseph of the Cambridge University Committee for Aerial Photography.

Leo Swan (1930–2001)

For his work on aerial photography at Tara, Leo Swan was acknowledged as one of 'the pioneers of Irish archaeology'.

Leo Swan initially trained as a teacher and later as an archaeologist. He was also interested in flying and spent some time working for the Flying Tigers, a squadron of American fighter pilots who fought in China during the Second World War. He undertook research, field survey and excavation, wrote for publication and gave lectures.

Leo Swan and Tara

Swan joined a flying club in County Meath, discovering many new monuments in the Leinster region. On one of these flights he took an aerial photograph of Tara, described in his obituary as 'probably the most significant aerial photograph in Irish archaeology'. Swan published an important article entitled 'The Hill of Tara, County Meath: the evidence of aerial photography,' in the *Journal of the Royal Society of Antiquaries of Ireland* in 1978, in which he included a number of ground-breaking photographs of Tara. He referred to Tara as 'perhaps the most enigmatic of our prehistoric sites'.

The Discovery Programme

Research on Tara entered a new era with the establishment of The Discovery Programme in 1991 by the then Taoiseach, Charles Haughey. The focus of study was initially the core period of Late Bronze Age/Iron Age, traditionally known as the 'Celtic' period.

Since the establishment of The Discovery Programme in 1991 there has been a return to the interdisciplinary study of Tara. The study of early Irish history, topography, literary sources, mythology, geophysical survey, mapping, measuring and 3D reconstructions all play a part in gaining an understanding of the monuments on Tara and its context in the wider landscape.

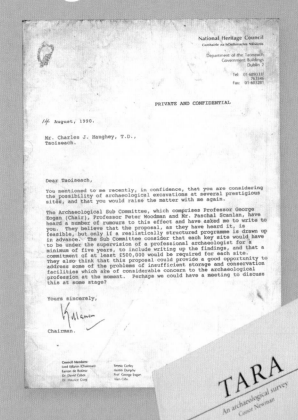

National Heritage Council
Comhairle na hOidhreachta Náisiúnta

Department of the Taoiseach
Government Buildings
Dublin 2

Tel: 01-609333/
763546
Fax: 01-603281

PRIVATE AND CONFIDENTIAL

14 August, 1990.

Mr. Charles J. Haughey, T.D.,
Taoiseach.

Dear Taoiseach,

You mentioned to me recently, in confidence, that you are considering the possibility of archaeological excavations at several prestigious sites, and that you would raise the matter with me again.

The Archaeological Sub Committee, which comprises Professor George Eogan (Chair), Professor Peter Woodman and Mr. Paschal Scanlan, have heard a number of rumours to this effect and have asked me to write to you. They believe that the proposal, as they have heard it, is feasible, but only if a realistically structured programme is drawn up in advance. The Sub Committee consider that each key site would have to be under the supervision of a professional archaeologist for a minimum of five years, to include writing up the findings, and that a commitment of at least £500,000 would be required for each site. They also think that this proposal could provide a good opportunity to address some of the problems of insufficient storage and conservation facilities which are of considerable concern to the archaeological profession at the moment. Perhaps we could have a meeting to discuss this at some stage?

Yours sincerely,

Chairman.

Council Members:
Lord Killanin (Chairman)
Eamon de Buitear
Dr. David Cabot
Dr. Maurice Craig
Teresa Corley
Austin Dunphy
Prof. George Eogan
Alan Gillis

TARA
An archaeological survey
Conor Newman

Discovery

THE IRISH TIMES, Saturday, May 11, 1991

National archaeological project begins

By Paul O'Neill

A MAJOR archaeological research and excavation programme was inaugurated yesterday by the Taoiseach, Mr Haughey. The project, which has a budget of £250,000 this year and £500,000 per annum in future years, would discover the past from the moment man first set foot in Ireland, he said.

The initiative, which is the fruit of Mr Haughey's personal vision, will involve the excavation of sites throughout the country. It was hailed as a "dream come true" by the UCD archaeologist, Professor George Eogan, who will chair the advisory panel which will formulate the "Discovery Programme" and supervise its implementation.

The list of sites for excavation has not been finalised but one already earmarked for development is the Hill of Tara in Co

Meath. Another being considered in Rath Cruacáin in Roscommon, while Mr Haughey emphasised his own interest in the islands off the west coast, which, he said, were very important in relation to the early Christian era.

He also said that the programme, which he first announced at the Fianna Fáil Ard-Fheis, would combine a professional archaeological approach with a popular dimension and would involve the "great institutes of learning around the world."

He added: "It will be totally scientific and professional. It will be designed and implemented to the highest professional archaeological standards so that it can stand up to world scrutiny. At the same time, we want it to supply information to the general public ... which will be incorporated into the curriculum in our

schools, information which will be made available to the public in the form of interpretative centres where necessary.

The project is being financed by the National Lottery funds via the Department of the Taoiseach. Mr Haughey said that no limit was being put on the programme — it could go on for five, 10 or 15 years. "The idea is that it will be all embracing and comprehensive, covering the whole country era by era. We want now to chart the whole thing so that from now on, all excavation will be part of this comprehensive approach."

The advisory panel, which met for the first time at the Department of the Taoiseach yesterday, is under the executive control of the Office of Public Works. The watchdog function of overseeing construction and development at archaeological sites will also remain with the OPW, although

Mr Haughey said the panel would be able to "sound the alarm" about projects.

Professor Eogan, a member of the National Heritage Council, said the story of Ireland would be covered from the beginning of human settlement down to the end of the early Christian period.

He also predicted spin-offs in terms of job creation and tourism and he said that work on at least one site would begin this year. On Tara, he said that despite the fact that it was well known, it was not at all understood archaeologically. Some limited work carried out in the 1950s showed that its history went back to the late Stone Age, although its heyday was during the Celtic period and it was one of the most comprehensive Celtic sites in Europe.

Professor Eogan said that the programme would enrich Euro-

pean archaeology as a because while Ireland wa island, its archaeology wa insular. "It's part and parc the great story of the emerg of European society," he ad

An international archaeolo has yet to be added to advisory panel. But in addition Professor Eogan, the other me bers include Professor Pete Woodman of UCC, Professo John Waddell of UCD, Dr Mike Baillie of Queen's University Professor Michael Herity of UCD, Dr Pat Wallace, director of the National Museum, Mr Pascal Scanlan of the National Heritage Council, Mr Noel Lynch of the OPW and Mr Anthony Cronin, the Taoiseach's cultural adviser.

Also present at the inaugural meeting yesterday was the chairman of the Heritage Council, Lord Killanin, and the chairman of the OPW, Mr John Mahoney.

Pushing the boundaries of science

A multi-disciplinary survey in the 1990s, using a combination of topographic, aerial, geophysical, geochemical and artefact studies, yielded new and interesting data and numerous archaeological monuments were discovered. Over 100,000m² was surveyed. The results were complemented by historical research.

Conor Newman and Joe Fenwick from
The Discovery Programme began the topographical
and geophysical surveys of Tara in the 1990s

Geophysical survey

The tools used in geophysical survey are different types of sensors. Archaeologists use ground-penetrating radar and magnetometers to obtain data. Geophysical survey could be likened to taking an x-ray through the hillside which reveals archaeological features under the surface. GIS has enabled archaeologists to discover new sites on the Hill of Tara and to reconstruct on a computer screen the wider archaeological landscape. This has revolutionized our understanding of Tara and provided new insights into the lives of our ancestors.

'Henge...we've found a henge!'

During the course of collaborative research between The Discovery Programme and NUI Galway, a massive henge was discovered using a fluxgate gradiometer, a device that measures anomalies in the earth's magnetic field caused by ground disturbance. This is very effective on a site like Tara as many of the archaeological features identified no longer have any surface traces.

Newspaper reports

'WOOD YOU BELIEVE IT? STONEHENGE FIND AT TARA'

Irish Independent, 11 April 2009

'For the first time, people will be able to view a computer-generated re-creation of what archaeologists believe was a major wooden structure – a version of Britain's Stonehenge – at the ancient seat of the Irish high kings in the Hill of Tara in Co. Meath'.

New technologies and new methodologies lead to ever-higher standards in archaeological field research. The equipment used to obtain data for the first computer generated models of the Hill of Tara included a total-station and a detail pole.

'"WOODHENGE" FOUND IN HILL OF TARA'S SOIL'

Sunday Times, 12 April 2009

'Ireland's Stonehenge, a 4,500-year-old structure at the Hill of Tara in Co. Meath, has been re-created by archaeologists and computer graphics experts. They have built a representation of a huge, wooden monument that appears to have been used for inauguration ceremonies and pagan burials of Ireland's high kings.'

Reconstruction of henge/ditched pit circle

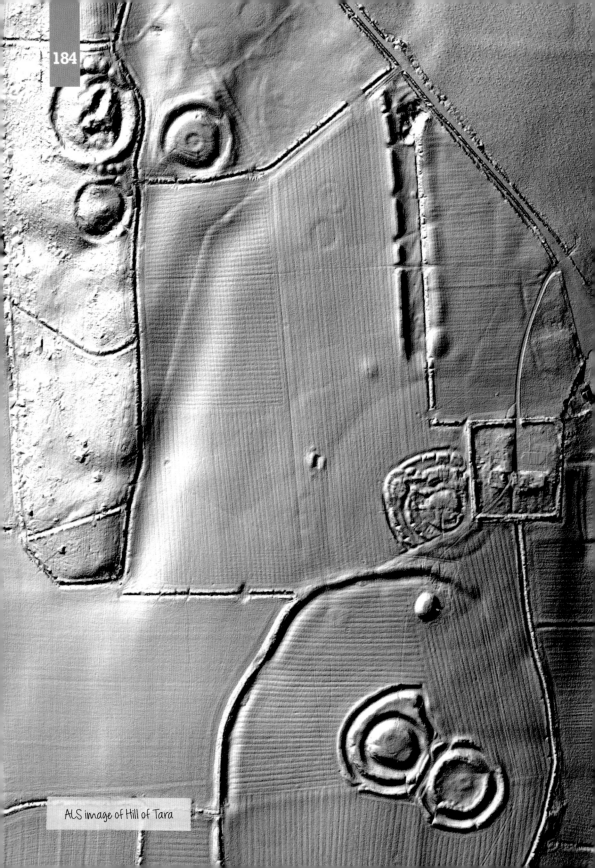

ALS image of Hill of Tara

Digital Terrain Model (DTM)

A DTM is a computer-generated three-dimensional representation of the physical shape of the ground surface.

Magnetometer

A magnetometer is an instrument used to measure the intensity of a magnetic field. Human activity such as burning or industrial activity changes the magnetic properties of soil.

ALS and 3D imaging

The most recent innovative technology used by The Discovery Programme includes Airborne Laser Scanning (ALS). Lasers are attached to a helicopter that flies over the archaeological site. They are used to scan height values over the ground surface, recording the data. This data can be used to generate 3D computer images of archaeological features that can be produced with or without the vegetation. A total area of 240ha was covered in the Tara ALS survey. This has proved to be a very practical and economic way of retrieving a large amount of information on an archaeological landscape without the expense or destruction of excavation.

Ger Dowling using a gradiometer

The National Roads Authority and Tara

One hundred and sixty-seven archaeological sites were excavated along the M3 Clonee to North of Kells motorway prior to its construction under the auspices of the National Roads Authority.

Harvesting the stars

One of the most important discoveries was the Iron Age Temple at Lismullin. It showed the importance of ritual monuments in the wider Tara landscape. One of the largest open-area excavations ever carried out by the state, it was undertaken by the archaeologist Aidan O'Connell of Archaeological Consultancy Services Limited and his team in 2007.

Early medieval sites

Early medieval settlement sites were discovered including Roestown, Baronstown and Castlefarm. The excavations at these large enclosed sites yielded very important information on how people in the medieval period lived. Early medieval cemetery sites were also discovered at Collierstown 1 and Ardsallagh.

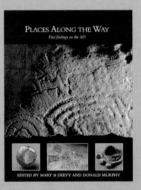

PLACES ALONG THE WAY
First findings on the M3

EDITED BY MARY B DEEVY AND DONALD MURPHY

Interdisciplinary study of Lismullin

Studies of archaeoastronomy, history and place-names provided a context. Scientific analysis of the soil to recreate the environment during the various periods of occupation was undertaken. These results combined with geophysics, Bayesian analysis, optically stimulated luminescence dating and an examination by specialists of the pottery

and metals all contributed to the final analysis of results and the interpretation of the site.

These were published by the National Roads Authority in a book in 2013 entitled *Harvesting the stars: a pagan temple at Lismullin, Co. Meath*.

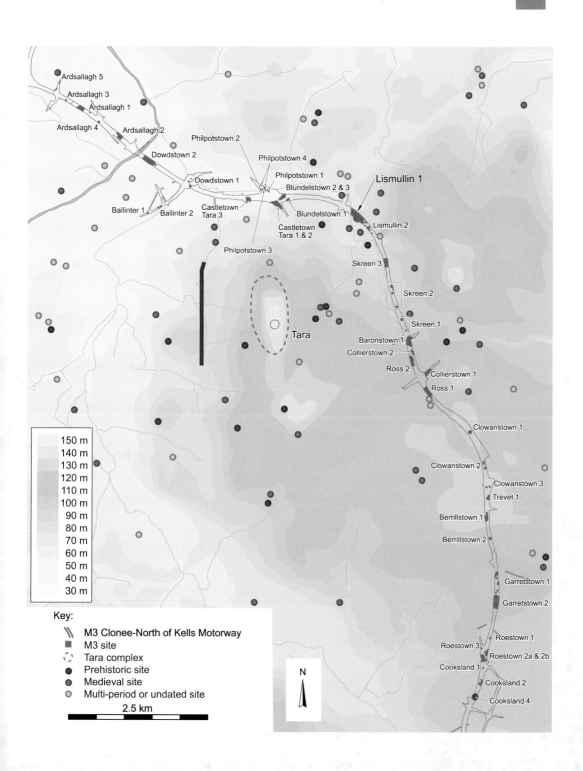

Ardsallagh 5
Ardsallagh 3
Ardsallagh 1
Ardsallagh 4
Ardsallagh 2
Dowdstown 2
Philpotstown 2
Philpotstown 4
Dowdstown 1
Philpotstown 1
Blundelstown 2 & 3
Lismullin 1
Castletown Tara 3
Ballinter 1
Ballinter 2
Blundelstown 1
Castletown Tara 1 & 2
Lismullin 2
Philpotstown 3
Skreen 3
Skreen 2
Skreen 1
Tara
Baronstown 1
Collierstown 2
Ross 2
Collierstown 1
Ross 1
Clowanstown 1
Clowanstown 2
Clowanstown 3
Trevet 1
Berrillstown 1
Berrillstown 2
Garretstown 1
Garretstown 2
Roestown 1
Roestown 3
Roestown 2a & 2b
Cooksland 1
Cooksland 2
Cooksland 4

150 m
140 m
130 m
120 m
110 m
100 m
90 m
80 m
70 m
60 m
50 m
40 m
30 m

Key:
M3 Clonee-North of Kells Motorway
M3 site
Tara complex
Prehistoric site
Medieval site
Multi-period or undated site

N

2.5 km

The mystery of Tara

Tara continues to fascinate archaeologists,
historians, scientists, anthropologists and
scholars of early Irish literature. While they
wrestle with the mysteries and meaning of
Tara, it is this very mystery that continues
to attract visitors from around the world.

Credits

Images:

Alamy Stock Images (www.alamy.com): pp 108, 133.

Alan Betson, *Irish Times*: Dáil sub-committee, p. 150.

An Post: 'St Patrick lights the Paschal fire at Slane', St Patrick's Day 2006 stamp by Sean Keating, p. 97 (reproduced by kind permission of An Post ©).

Annie West (www.anniewest.com): illustrations, pp 22–3, 25, 32, 68–9, 71, 78, 104–5, 116, 119, 120, 128–130, 139, 154.

British Library: medieval wedding (Royal 6 E VI, f. 375), p. 109.

Campaign to save Tara (www.campaigntosavetara.blogspot.ie): aerial photograph, p. 151.

Candyland (www.candyland.ecrater.com): chess set, p. 30.

Century Magazine: 'Cú Chulainn riding his chariot into battle' by J.C. Leyendecker (1907), p. 81.

Chapel of the Novitiate of the Oblate Fathers of St Mary Immaculate, Belcamp, Co. Dublin: Eithne and Fedelm window by Harry Clarke, p. 100.

Cló Mhaigh Eo: front cover of *Dhá Chluas Capaill ar Labhraí Loingseach* by Eithne Ní Ghallchobhair, p. 27.

Department of the Environment, Northern Ireland: aerial photograph, p. 82.

Des Mooney: Lia Fáil at sunrise, p. 37.

Dundalgan Press: drawing of skeleton from *Tara: the monuments on the hill* by Seán P. Ó Ríordáin, p. 51.

Eamhain Mhacha Heritage Apps (navanfortapp.com): Navan Fort reconstruction, p. 83.

Eamonn Farrell, Photocall Ireland: Lia Fáil and memorial stone, 1798, p. 135.

English Heritage: Stonehenge Cursus, p. 43.

Eric Luke, *Irish Times*: Niall of the Nine Hostages, p. 91.

Flickr: Hochdorf gold shoes (Xuan Che), p. 36; Mound of the Hostages (shakeyblakey), p. 44; Evie Hone window, p. 141.

Freemasons' Hall: Crest of the Grand Lodge, Freemasons' Hall, p. 145.

Heritage Council: Letter from Lord Killanin to C.J. Haughey, 14 August 1990, p. 180.

Igor Oleynikov: Salmon of Knowledge, p. 72.

Illustrated London News: Daniel O'Connell on Tara, 15 Aug 1843, p. 136.

Indymedia Ireland (www.indymedia.ie): pp 122, 130, 152.

Inghinidhe na hÉireann (1905–6): p. 139.

Jan Pospisil (www.merlkir.deviantart.com): Anglo-Saxon burial, p. 99.

Jean-Louis Brunaux: Gournay-sur-Aronde, p. 75.

Jim Fitzpatrick (www.jimfitzpatrick.com): 'Lugh rides to Battle', p. 30 and 'Sadb', p. 33.

Joe Fenwick, NUIG: Rathcroghan, pp 16, 84.

John Barrett: Tara at sunrise, pp 18–19.

John Duncan: Lia Fáil, p. 12.

John Quigley (artist) and Paula Geraghty (photographer): 'Save Tara valley' human sculpture, p. 156.

Jonathan Hession: pp 49–50, 53, 132.

Leo Swan: aerial photograph, p. 179.